The People's History

Chester-le-Street

The Twentieth Century

by

Dorothy A. Hall & George Nairn

Chester-le-Street's Home Guard in 1944. Colonel Len Usher was the commanding officer. The Home Guard was on duty in January 1941 when there was a Messerschmitt 109 exhibited in the cricket field. The exhibition raised £40 for the Spitfire Fund. Four months earlier had seen the worst local incident of the war when bombs were dropped at Beamish. The next day local people invaded the area to see the damage and collection boxes were put out. Twelve pounds, mainly in coppers, was collected for the Spitfire Fund.

Previous page: Workmen employed by William Middleton, joiner and builder, of South Burns. The Middletons, like the Kells, were a long established Chester-le-Street family trading not only as stone masons, joiners but also publicans. William Middleton was at the Joiner's Arms in South Burns for 28 years.

Copyright © Dorothy A. Hall & George Nairn 1999

First published in 1999 by

The People's History Ltd
Suite 1
Byron House
Seaham Grange Business Park
Seaham
Co. Durham
SR7 0PY

ISBN 1 902527 04 6

Contents

Chester-le-Street Town Band, winners of the 1899 Tynemouth Palace Challenge cup. Included are, back row: J. Gardiner, H. Ayling, J. Cairns, Deighton Reed, J. Herring. Third row: J. Williams, A. Howarth, S. Wake, R. Lambert, G.H. Wright, J. Hughes, T. Pick, T. Lambert, Dennis Jude. Second row: J. Layton, Frank Bruce, J. Pattison, P.H. Stoddart, W. Taylor, G. Rogerson, Archie Scott, R. Boyd. Front row: G Ritchie, J. Forster, Thomas Jude, Peter Batey, T.R. Holliday, John Brown, W. Harle and Edward Dawson. In 1898 the patroness of the band was the Countess of Scarbrough and the President was Sir Lindsay Wood. Vice Presidents included: the Earl of Scarbrough, The Rector, Sir James Joicey, Dr William Renton, C.R. Barrett, J.W. Luccock and a long list of others. The five guineas donated by Sir Lindsay headed the subscription list. The Town Band disbanded in 1919 following a dispute over their non-appearance at the town's Peace Celebrations.

Front cover: Clarence Terrace Nursery, *circa* 1949, with Joseph Citrone at the far right of the see-saw.

Introduction

In my attic, as well as books, photographs, pieces of carpet and countless other items, there are odds and ends of Chester-le-Street's history. There is a bit of blue plaster from the Star Hall, Horner's tins with Dainty Dinah pictured as well as the later Coronation tin and others from Kenneth Horner's time. I have all the paper work to do with the 1851 Census book. There's a Cestrian Mallow tin made in High Chare and a Victorian tray where the ladies and others left their calling cards – bought from Usher's salesrooms. There are books I have picked up over the years – Hylton Gray's report book for the years 1928 to 1933 signed by J.J. Simms. There is Sarah Thornton's First Prize book at the Burns School in 1914 signed by Alured de Moleyns. And that's just up in the attic!

I am not a Cestrian but in the last 33 years that I have known the town I have come to love its history and its people. George born and bred here is a Cestrian through and through. George and I first met through postcards of Chester-le-Street and our joint passion for the 'City of the World' led us to meet Jack and Nancy Stoker. Together they shared their memories and, as they got to know us, their rich store of postcards and photographs. Jack and I published a postcard book together in 1987. In 1999 George and I would like to dedicate this book to the memory of Jack and Nancy Stoker. For without their hoarding many of these photographs would have been lost forever.

Dorothy A. Hall

Kathryn Iicyszyn from St Cuthbert's RC School presented a bouquet to the Queen watched by Don Robson Cricket Club Chairman and County Council Leader and Prince Philip at the opening of the Riverside development in October 1995.

Acknowledgements

Out thanks go to the people named below for the use of their photographs. If we have used your photograph and not acknowledged you, our apologies and thanks. If we have got the facts, dates or names wrong please contact us – the next edition can be altered! Thank you Dorothy Rand for proof reading our notes. Finally we both thank our partners, Alan and Gillian. They do put up with our fascination with Chester-le-Street.

Beamish Photographic Archive, Cestrian Flower Club, Chester-le-Street District Council, Chester-le-Street Town FC, Chester-le-Track, Kibblesworth Primary School Archive, North East Press Sunderland Echo Ltd, Mr and Mrs Alan Bailey, M. Blenkinsop, Miss Bloomfield, Mr and Mrs Bowman, Mrs Brown, Margaret Caygill, Josie Citrone, Mary Citrone, Mr and Mrs E. Collings, Jean Copeman, Mrs Dodds, Mrs Emmerson, Mrs Fowle, Tony Golightly, Claire and Gillian Hall, T. Harvey, Alan Hedley, Mr and Mrs D. Henderson, Ruby Hodgson, Nancy Holden, Eric Howard, Mr and Mrs W. Hurworth, Mary Kell, Mr Leedale, Judith Lees, Misses Louth, Nigel Marsh, Mrs Moffat, Mary Mossop, Olive Murrell, Mrs Punshon, Gavin Purdon, Rachel Ramsey, Mary Robinson, Janet Robson, Mrs Ryan, Colin Saunders, Jimmy Small, Mr and Mrs Smithson, Lionel and Marion Stoker, Mrs Frankie Thompson, R. Watson, Mrs S. Wears, George Weatherley, Joyce Whitmore.

Chester-le-Street is often pictured as a town serving the surrounding mining area. However, it was not until the 1950s that the cattle market held fortnightly ceased. Pictured here is one of the October horse sales at Turnbull's Auction Mart in Station Road. Paddy's Market was held here every Friday afternoon and all day Saturday in the years between the wars and until the market in the Burns opened in 1957.

THE DAWN OF THE CENTURY

The River Wear provided entertainment for many generations of Cestrians.
Amateur Swimming Club competitions and regattas were popular on a
summer's evening. Here are a group of lady swimmers on the banks of the
Wear.

Thomas Elliott's Tailor Costumier Hatter and Hosiery shop was on the corner of Ivanhoe Terrace and Relton Terrace. Thomas Elliott was in Finchdale Road in 1902, but by 1906 had moved to Durham Road. A section of the shop was opened as a Post Office. The Post Box was cleared: 8.30 am, 10.30 am and also at 2.10, 6.00, 8.30 and 10.15 pm, Sundays 6 pm. In 1919 the Luccock family had a house in Relton Terrace.

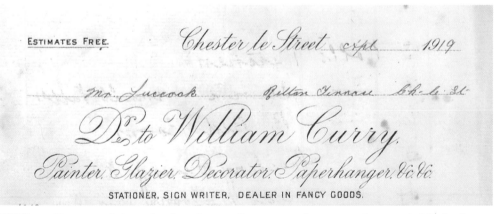

William Curry, painter, glazier, decoration, paperhanger, a long established firm in the town papered and painted a whole house in Relton Terrace for £27 5 shillings. (This included the wallpaper!) Curry's continued in business until the 1980s.

The Shrove Tuesday Football game whose origins are lost in time was a real event in the 1900s. Up Streeters and Down Streeters (the demarcation line being Low Chare) gathered for the one o'clock pancake bell and waited for the throwing out of the ball. The Murray family had provided and thrown out the ball for most of the nineteenth century. Members of the family returned for the Shrove Tuesday game even after they had left Chester-le-Street. There were no goals – the object of the game to have the ball north or south of Low Chare. At six o'clock the ball was returned to the donor and the winners announced usually from the upstairs of a public house. These are the winners in 1903.

This early photograph of Shrove Tuesday shows an unusual view of the Burns and the lower end of Front Street. The ball often found its way into the Cone and was lost. There was usually more than one ball. For most of the latter years of the century the balls had been made by Dalkin's the saddlers. They were made in eight parts laced together with a natural bladder inside. The Congregational Church held a Shrove Tuesday meeting and tea.

Members of Chester-le-Street Cycling Club taken at the turn of the century on Mains Park Road. This area has seen many changes and the houses at the corner of Church Chare contain Blythe's Birtley bricks dated 1896. The Deanery gatehouse can be seen and in the background the Parish Church of St Mary and St Cuthbert.

The Deanery is pictured here with the Church in the background. Durham County Education Committee bought the house and site of $2^{1}/_{2}$ acres for £2,000. T.F. Brass Esq, County Councillor, Chair of Governors, who was a colliery agent from Sacriston, officially opened the Secondary School on the 19th September 1911. The new school building was built with bricks from Pelaw, stone dressing from Gateshead Fell and Westmorland slates. Since its beginnings in the Mechanics Institute in 1905, the school has had only seven head teachers: R. Sanderson 1905-16, F. Munford 1916-20, J.J. Simms 1920-34, J. Smailes 1934-64, Dr E.J. Dunston 1964-73, P. Driscoll 1974-90 and A.M. Thompson 1990 to date.

The Deanery was the home of Lieutenant Colonel Edward Johnson JP from 1830 until his death in 1885. After that John William Luccock lived there. These photographs are of Mr Luccock and of one of the Deanery rooms taken in Mr Luccock's time. Whellan's 1894 Directory tells us that J.W. Luccock's were wholesale manufacturing confectioners as well as butter and cheese importers, whilst Kelly's Directory for 1894 tells us that this was at the Stag Steam Works. (Luccock was later to have a jam factory on this site on Foundry Lane).

The Osborne Working Men's Club bought a house on Osborne Road from John Turnbull in September 1904 for £1,200. The years since have seen many alterations and extensions but the original building can still be seen. This photograph is of members taken in the early part of the century. James Turnbull and Son had been established in 1879 and were auctioneers, valuers and land agents. Turnbull's had telephone number 1 in 1906. James Turnbull lived in Springfield House, Mains Park Road and John Turnbull lived in Mains House on the Front Street in 1902.

This is an early photograph of St Cuthbert's Roman Catholic Church in Ropery Lane. The Church was opened in 1910 costing about £5,000. The building was of local stone and could seat 350. It replaced the Catholic School Chapel, which had been built in 1888

although Catholic meetings had taken place prior to this in the Mechanics' Institute from 1881.

Church and Chapel still had much influence in Chester-le-Street at the turn of the century. In 1898 the whole of the debt for the Primitive Methodist Schoolrooms (opened in 1886) seen at the rear of this photograph was cleared and 'without pause' funds began to be raised for the completion of the site and the building of the Church. Prospect House had belonged to the Murray family.

Sir James Joicey Bart MP later Lord Joicey (1906) was Liberal Member of Parliament for Chester-le-Street from 1885 to 1906. He laid the foundation stone for the Central Methodist Chapel on 18th September 1901. Sir James was followed as Member of Parliament by John Wilson Taylor 1906-19, Jack Lawson 1919-49, Patrick Bartley 1950-55, Norman Pentland 1956-73 and Giles Radice 1974 to date.

8th October 1902 saw the official opening of the Central Church by W.P. Hartley Esq JP. The building had cost £3,300. Pictured here are the completed Church and Miss Lydia Curry with the official key from the opening. The debts were a constant reason for fund-raising including 'Ye Olde Chester-le-Street Bazaar' held at the Mechanics' Institute, 28th, 29th, and 30th November 1911 whose object was to raise £500 towards the reduction of the debt of £1,500. The Earl of Durham opened the bazaar. The brochure for the bazaar details stalls, entertainment and children's programmes.

The Congregational Church or Bethel Church in Low Chare originally built in 1814 was improved in 1860 by the heightening of the roof, the addition of an organ gallery and new pews. In 1882 further alterations were made. By the turn of the century the Church hoped to move to a new site on Front Street. However this was not to be and the Church remains in Low Chare. The Brotherhood formed in Rev J.G. Williams' time (1907-10) continued until 1961.

Congregational Church

This photograph, taken in the Rectory Gardens, shows one of the many amateur dramatic shows organised by the Church. The Church magazine for August 1906 gives details of the Church life at this time. There is the Sunday School treat when 400 children assembled at the school in Low Chare and marched to Mr Kerrich-Walker's field. A concert and comedietta was being held at the Co-op Hall. The Choir, Sunday School teachers and the Church Committee were going on a trip to South Shields by rail. The Church Lads were at camp at Warkworth. Other outings included trips to Whitby, Redcar, Roker and Finchale. A busy summer for the Church.

Back Chare showing the high wall of the Deanery gardens at the turn of the century. This was to be the site of the first Council Schools. The Church had provided the schools in the town since 1842. The Burns Infants built in 1876, the Victoria 1888 and finally the Infant School being built in 1902. However, the passing of the 1902 Education Act, giving responsibility to County Councils for elementary education, led to the building of the Church Chare Boys and Girls' Schools in 1909. The head teachers in 1909 were Miss J.K. Dancaster and Mr T.B. Hall. The Rector Rev de Moleyns writing in the Church Magazine April 1909 said, 'Let me then strongly urge all Church parents to show who values the soul more than the body to still keep their children at our schools, where besides given as good a secular education, we will also try to instil the truth of the Gospel … "

Stonemasons were an important part of the trade's history of the town and none more so than the Kell family. An advertisement for John Kell and Son (below) shows the range of his work and the photograph taken at the monumental mason's yard shows a number of his employees. The cemetery in Ropery Lane was opened 1st August 1895 and was built by Kell and Groves. John Kell promised to provide the first headstone for the new graveyard – the first entry is a stillborn baby and the second entry is for his own son Joseph who died on the 9th August.

SECTION TWO

THE GREAT WAR

The Road To Glory, Lambton Park.

'The Road to Glory' was written 26th July 1915. The message reads: 'The riders are just going on a route march.' This postcard cost 2d from Clarke's the Printers. By this time the news from the front was less cheerful and the *Chronicle* lists the wounded, missing and killed men from all over the Chester-le-Street district.

A delivery cart in front of the main premises of the Co-operative Store, *circa* 1910. Chester-le-Street Co-operative and Industrial Society Limited celebrated its Golden Jubilee 7th-10th August 1912. A brochure on the History and Handbook of arrangements in connection with the Jubilee was published by the Co-operative Printing Society of Newcastle. The 64-page book includes photographs of Joseph Bruce, president, John Pringle, general secretary, William Hepworth, cashier, Walter Black, general manager and the past and present management committees. The history details the early days of the society from the beginnings in November 1862 in the back room of one of the founders, to the purchasing of the site on Front Street in 1869 for £1,200. Later, new shops were built on the site. The Co-operative Society expanded with further premises being built in 1886 together with 31 houses in Co-operative Street. Every member was presented, on production of their store passbook, with an art copper tray suitably inscribed and with views of the Central and principal Branch Premises as a Jubilee Souvenir in August 1912.

Right: Cud Liddle. In the days before radios, television and daily newspapers the billposter was an essential means of telling people what was happening in the town. There had been various Bellmen such as J. Watson and G. Young at the end of the century. Cuthbert or Cud Liddle was well known in the 1910s as a bill distributor. He lived in Hopgarth and went missing in February 1916. Nine weeks later his body was found in the River Wear at Sunderland. The Inquest, which followed, reached an open verdict.

The front hall of Whitehill Hall in about 1910. Until his death in 1917, Whitehill Hall was the home of Charles Rollo Barrett, mining engineer and coal owner. Whitehill Hall had been the Cookson residence for many years. In 1892 C.R. Barrett came to assist his brother-in-law, Sir Lindsay Wood, in connection with the colliery interests of the Ecclesiastical Commissioners in the north. Pelton Colliery Company acquired the land at Whitehill. There were subsidence problems and the house was declared unsafe in 1917. A window in the Parish Church is dedicated to the memory of C.R. Barrett and his son Lindsay, killed in 1916.

Right: This is a photograph of Doris Crawford on Violet Day – when 40,000 pennies (£166) were needed to purchase the first motor ambulance. In May 1919 Mr J.T. Saunders suggested that a motor ambulance could be acquired for the town. Later it was arranged that it could be housed at Picktree Lane Garage. The ambulance arrived September 1919 – in case of emergency just ring 15. The ambulance could take 4 stretchers or 12 people seated. Tommy Hardy drove for the Ambulance Committee for 46 years.

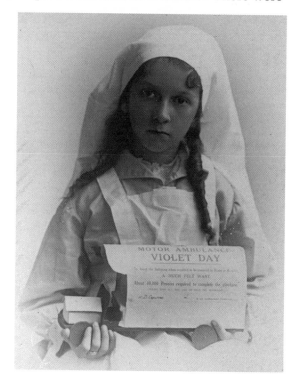

These two views of the Brewery in South Burns are unusual as not many photographs of this area have survived. In the 1910s Youngers continued brewing for its own houses and customers. The Great War brought in new restrictions. August 1914 saw public houses closing from 9 pm to 8 am. January 1915 saw the Government introducing the New Licensing Act. Sunday opening was restricted to 12.30 to 2.30 and 6.00 to 9.00. The long pull continued to cause problems and in June 1916 came the news that brewers were to cut production by 15% and that no beer was to be imported. However, drunkenness problems persisted and the *Chester Chronicle* of 9th February 1917 reads: 'In spite of cutting the drinking hours from 17 to 5 cases of drunkenness have not fallen especially amongst women.'

1911 saw the Suffragette movement come to Chester-le-Street. A meeting was held in the library of the Church Institute. Concerts were organised although the one in late December 1911 was not well attended. The Chester-le-Street group held their first annual meeting in June 1912. A suffragette bomb was found at the Cricket Pavilion in June 1913 – written on the tin was 'Votes for Women'. This photograph shows a group of amateur swimmers including 2 suffragettes – possibly males. So perhaps the people of Chester-le-Street did not take the suffragette movement too seriously!

Luccock's factory was taken over by J. Samuel in the early 1900s. The change of company name from J. Samuel to George W. Horner took place on 12th October 1910. The next ten years were to see Horner's company expand. In 1911 Horner's were advertising: 'Smart Girls over 18 for weighing up of sweets and for jar washers, wages 12 shillings per week.' Horner's also produced Aunt Mary's baking range and in 1911 ran a baking competition for Aunt Mary's sponge sandwich and drop cakes in the Congregational Schoolroom. A lady's watch was the first prize.

By 1919 Horner's employed 770 females and 107 males. Mermaid Toffee, the forerunner of Dainty Dinah, was a favourite of local troops during the Great War. Meanwhile at home there was the Dainty Dinah AFC, a woman's football team. In April 1918 they played and were beaten 6-0 by Angus Sanderson's team at Durham.

DAINTY DINAH'S AFC

FRONT STREET, CHESTER-LE-STREET, ON SHROVE TUESDAY. Nº 1

Shrove Tuesday football was an annual feature of Chester-le-Street life. Both these postcards are dated 1911. The first shows the preparations needed before the game commenced and the second shows the crowd gathering outside Clarke's shop. A gentleman can be seen standing on a balcony. Mr W. Clarke, Tom Burn of the Lambton Arms and latterly Mrs Dalkin had thrown out the ball. 1913 sees the beginnings of rumblings about the cost (£100) of the barricades and the damage done to the window frames. 1914 brought the problems of Northern buses. Front Street was closed and buses north bound had to stand at the Primitive Methodist chapel, south bound at Ropery Lane. The Scottish Horse, training at Chester-le-Street during the Great War, were out on manoeuvres in 1915 and missed the fun. By 1916 no joinery firm had men to spare and wood was scarce. It was not until 1920 that Shrove Tuesday football returned to the street.

This photograph was taken in 1910 to commemorate the first local peal of *Treble Bob Major* rung in the Parish Church on June 13th 1910 by John Crawford, James Anderson, George Siddle, Anthony Meyers, William Brown, George Albert Ward, Frederick Sheraton and James Robinson.

The Parish Church Choir taken on the side steps of the Church in 1918. The incumbent at the time was Rev Alured Bayfield de Moleyns, rector from 1895-1919. The two curates are: F.H. Harrison and A.D.E. Titcombe. Choirboys included: J. Sewell, R. Legg, J. Robson, G. Guy, and J. Crawford. The gentleman at the top left of the stairs is Sir Lindsay Wood of the Hermitage. Sir Lindsay died on 22nd September 1920.

The Secondary School had been officially opened in 1911 and in the next few years numerous references are found in the *Chester Chronicle*. From 1912 all new pupils had to pass an entrance examination. The school also ran a large number of evening classes including technical classes in Practical Maths, Hand-sketching, Geometry, Elementary Mechanics, Physics and English. Whilst commercial classes included Shorthand, Commercial Arithmetic, Typewriting and Office Routines. There were Building Trade, Mining, Domestic and Preparatory courses available in 1911. Here we see the avenue of fine trees and the tennis courts in the school grounds as well as the girls' cricket team from about this time.

Secondary School, Chester-le-Street Avenue and Tennis Ground

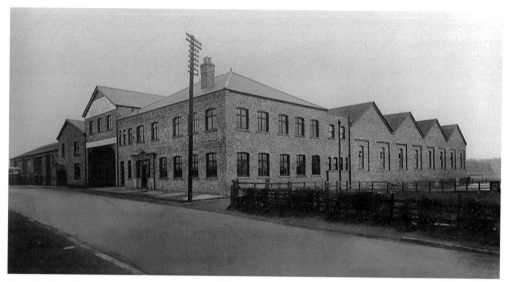

The first mention of a motor bus scheme linking Chester-le-Street and Low Fell is in the *Chester Chronicle* for May 1912. The bus depot in Picktree Lane (above) was put out to tender in November 1912. Mr B. Bolam of Birtley was the successful builder and by March it was making rapid progress. The garage had one of the earliest systems of underground petrol storage systems – the Bywater Hydraulic – with a capacity of 3,500 gallons. The first bus chassis were made by Straker and Squire of Bristol and the bodies by Imisch and Co of London. Newspaper advertisements detailed times and fares – 'The Company cannot be responsible for delays.'

The *Chester Chronicle* records that it was at 2 o'clock to the minute on 7th May 1913 that the first Northern General Transport Bus Company bus left the bottom of Chester-le-Street for Low Fell. The double-decker bus was quite full. A ten-minute service continued the rest of the day. The whole journey cost 5d, $2^1/2$d to Birtley. 'Bus fever'

struck Chester-le-Street – the whole fleet and all the staff was out. Two weeks later an advert instructs passengers to signal by raising a hand when wishing to enter the bus. A leader soon asks 'Why not a service up Front Street?' and 'Why not a trip to Finchale on a Wednesday in the summer?' Already 47 people had been taken by bus to Pelton Fell one Saturday night. The bus service rapidly expanded to the many villages in the area. By January 1914 there was a fleet of 27 buses based at Chester-le-Street.

An advert for the Chester-le-Street Printing Company. With W. Clarke proprietor, the company commenced publication of the *Chester-le-Street Chronicle* on 19th August 1911. For the next 24 years the *Chronicle* brought weekly to the people of the district the news both big and small. It advertised itself: 'As the paper, which enters every home.' The newspapers are fascinating documents detailing Chester-le-Street's history, which have been and will continue to be used as a rich source of information.

Chester=le=Street Printing Co.

(WM. CLARKE, Proprietor).

Artistic and . General Printers, &c. .

Bookbinders, Stationers, Relief . Stampers, Engravers.

X Entrance to Printing Works through Stationery Shop.

Front Street (Foot of Station Lane).

The *Chester-le-Street Chronicle* for 7th August 1914 says: 'This country is involved in one of the most immense struggles that it has ever had to face.' The next four years were to bring hardship and heart ache for all Cestrians. Two hundred men had already left the town by 7th August. Lambton Park was to be the training base for a number of regiments. Whilst Chester-le-Street town was invaded by 4,500 Scottish Horse soldiers. The officers stayed at the Queen's Head and Kings Head. The Lambton Arms was the headquarters of the Commanding officer, Colonel Farquahar. The men were billeted in the Council Schools. The *Chronicle* laments the fact that Chester has no public baths! Postcards such as this one were popular. This card sent to Miss Cooke of Macclesfield by her brother Albert. He is more concerned about whether the family had gathered the hay in.

'Greetings from Lambton Park' gives the names of some of the troops – The Denbighs, Cheshires, RAMC. The card reads, 'We are ready for the front now. I think we will be going shortly.' We do not know what happened to the sender, H. Boyes.

A halt on the Great North Road shows an unusual shot of the cottages which were on North Road between Blind Lane Roundabout and the entrance to Longdean Park.

The Great War cut across society; the Earl of Durham lost one of his brothers and his nephew, Sir Lindsay Wood his son Collingwood. C.R. Barrett's son, Lindsay, pictured here was killed 17th March 1916. At the Secondary School 3 masters, the caretaker and 130 old boys had died. The *Chester Chronicle* for 15th November 1918 reads: 'Tidings of Peace – the whole town was soon decked with flags and streamers across the Front Street but much sorrow tinged the gladness. Many people have lost loved ones.'

This photograph from the *Chester Chronicle* is of John Hurworth killed in action, found in the field 26th September 1915. He was the son of John and Isabella Hurworth of Chester-le-Street. John was a Private in the Durham Light Infantry. He has no known grave and is commemorated on the Menin Gate Memorial at Ypes. John Hurworth is the great uncle of George Nairn. Lindsay Barrett was a Major in the First Battalion of the Northumberland Fusiliers. He has a window in the Parish Church dedicated to his memory and is buried at Poperinge, West Vlaanderen, Belgium. Both John and Lindsay are on the memorials inside and outside the Parish Church.

CHESTER-LE-STREET WESLEYAN SUNDAY SCHOOL.

Sunday School Anniversaries were a feature of the Methodist year. Learning your pieces, practising the choruses and hopefully having new clothes to wear, all went to make them very special occasions. In the 1910s demonstrations were popular and these two photographs of Station Road Chapel, taken in 1912 and 1914 are good examples.

CHESTER LE STREET WESLEYAN SUNDAY SCHOOL. MAY 17. 1914.

YOURS SINCERELY.

VALENTINE VIVIAN,

ELOCUTIONIST, VOCALIST, HUMOURIST, AND
LECTURER, OPEN TO ENGAGEMENTS FOR WHOLE
OR PART EVENINGS.

Valentine Vivian was a stonemason by trade but was ousted from his craft partly by the introduction of machinery. He toured the United States and Canada as a Temperance Lecturer. He also toured England as an actor. These are adverts he used. He was a resident of Chester-le-Street for a number of years and was employed by the Co-operative Society and lived in 207 Front Street – the Co-op's South Branch. Valentine played an active part in politics. He held strong socialist opinions. He died in February 1912 aged 54. Rev J.G. Soulsby of Birtley conducted the funeral service at the cemetery. The coffin was borne by employees of the Co-op. In attendance were representatives of Chester-le-Street Co-operative Society, Employees Union of County Council evening Classes, the Brotherhood and the Divisional Labour Party.

South Pelaw Colliery Welfare Football team in about 1910. Dickson Weatherly was the goalkeeper. Mr Corker of Emmanuel House, Hilda Terrace is on the left. Park View houses are behind the team. William Corker had a general shop at South Pelaw for many years. He was well known as a pig and poultry breeder. When he died in 1935 he had been a director of a local picture company. His daughter and grand-daughters continued with the shop. The last family member broke with tradition in 1992 and the business was transferred out of the Corker family. The shop continues to be known as Corker's.

THE CHARLESTON
YEARS

The Victoria Boys football team, season 1922-23, taken at the school. Back row: Mr W.U. Cuthbertson, Mr Summers (trainer), Chris Robinson, Frankie Birse, Harry Wales, Eddie Piggford, Billy Wales, Harry James, Mr Pearson and Mr Airey. Front row: Jimmy Malcolm, George Tewart, Eddie Wake, Tom Thorogood and Billy Jamfrey. Eddie Piggford is wearing a County cap. 'Haway the Vix put the ball through the sticks' was the battle cry of the football team.

Dr A. Cecil Renton (right) passed away at his residence Castle View in January 1927. Dr Renton had been born in 1888 at St Mary's House. He joined his father in practice in 1912. Active service followed in Mesopotamia at No 1 British General Hospital where he was given the temporary rank of Major in the RAMC. He was a clever physician and a brilliant surgeon. Dr Renton's last journey to the Parish Church saw the street from Castle View entrance to the Church lined with thousands of people. Business was suspended and the blinds of all the houses and shops in the town were drawn. This photograph was a supplement to the *Chester Chronicle* of 21st January 1927. Over the next year various ideas for a memorial to Dr Renton were put forward; however the only memorial we have found is a stone plaque on the side of the War Memorial.

Chester-le-Street's famous twins, Joseph and Jack Bainbridge featured at many public occasions in the 1920s. They were present when the New Zealand cricket team came to Chester-le-Street. Here we see them at one of the carnivals held in the town to raise money for the Poor Children's Treat. The identical twins born in 1844 had come to Pelton Fell when young and had worked at the Pelton Fell pit from the age of 12 until they were 70 years of age. The twins were inseparable companions and both enjoyed a large measure of good health and were great walkers – although they never walked together. Joseph died in March 1929 and Jack three months later.

The War Memorial, Chester-le-Street. (b)

A month before the official opening of the Town's War Memorial, at a cost of between £500 and £600, there was still a debt of £50. The Committee led by Mr J.T. Saunders was anxious that the memorial should be opened free of debt. The publicity in the *Chronicle* led to the money being raised. On 15th February 1925, 3000 spectators watched the unveiling of the War Memorial at the north end of town. The memorial was in the Renaissance style of the Doric order 32

feet by 13 feet with an open terrace, with seats for the aged people of the town. Mr John Lant, of Newcastle, prepared the stonework. Mr Ralph Hedley, also of Newcastle, executed the massive shield over the central arch. The shield represented a St George's cross surmounted by a crown and draped with foliage. Beneath the shield was the Latin inscription 'Pro Patria' – 'For Their Country'. On a white marble tablet were the names of 262 of Chester-le-Street's illustrious dead.

Chester-le-Street War Memorial. (5324)

The Armistice in 1918 brought forward many suggestions of Welcome Home Schemes and Memorials – a cottage hospital, houses for the widows of soldiers, park and recreational grounds and finally a new memorial hall. However, it was the Parish Church who made plans for a war memorial as early as May 1919. The unveiling by Sir Arthur N.L. Wood and the dedication by the Bishop of Durham took place on 26th February 1922.

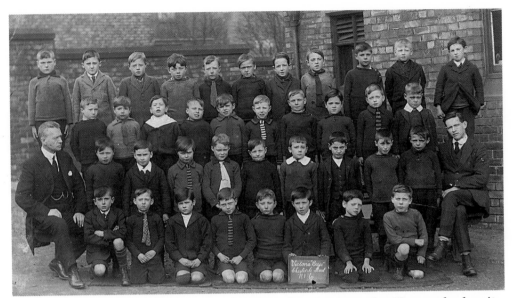

The Victoria Church of England Boys' School in Co-operative Terrace had as its headmaster from 1903, when he succeeded his brother, Captain William Usher Cuthbertson. He had a wasted arm and Miss Roscamp, a member of staff, recalled having to help him on with his coat. Captain Cuthbertson was Colour Sergeant of the Northern Cyclist Battalion who were at camp when the Great War broke out. He remained to take charge of the Mayor of Morpeth's army and drilled them till they joined Kitchener's army. Earlier Cuthbertson had entered local politics and his newspaper campaign ran: 'For whom should the working man vote? Who has watched him grow from boy to man? CUTHBERTSON. Who has encouraged his manly sports? CUTHBERTSON.' He was elected to the Urban District Council in May 1914 for the Chester ward but did not stand after this. He is seen here on the left of the photograph. The teacher was G. Garside. Boys include: Jack Bailey, Piggford, Albert Wales, Bobby Brown and Thomas Hornsby.

Dating back to the days when early closing day in the town was a Wednesday, 12 o'clock – this is a photograph of the Chester-le-Street Tradesmen's cricket team of 1925. They were joint holders of the Tyneside Wednesday Shield in 1929. Cricket matches  were played in the cricket field off Mains Park Road and the team continued to play at Chester-le-Street for 53 years until 1967 when they were asked to leave because of heavy club demands and county and club calls.

The Burns area in the 1920s showing an early Northern omnibus, a travellers' caravan, Moles building, Canada to the right and just visible the Maltings in front of the viaduct. The open river Cone can also be seen. The Northern General Transport Co Ltd by 1924 had depots at Sunderland, Bensham, Stanley, Consett as well as the Picktree Lane Garage and Offices. Chester-le-Street was well provided with other bus services. Buses from humble 6 seater Fords to comfortable 30 seater Leviathans were supplied by H. Young (Motors) Ltd, Front Street, Chester-le-Street.

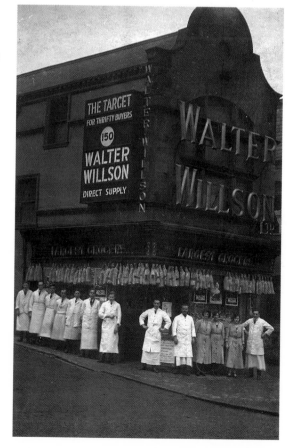

Walter Willson's staff pictured outside their shop below the Queen's Head about 1923. The manager at that time was Mr G. Hetherington. Walter Willson's moved into Chester-le-Street in the 1880s and remained in the town until about 1985. In 1999 Walter Willson's were taken over and all their records given to Beamish Museum. A copy of this photograph was included and the employees are named from left to right: Cyril Slater, A. Petrie, J. Ethrington, W. Clark, H. Hodgson, O. Cunningham, ? Coulson, G. Hetherington, J. Vitress, Miss E. Pinkney, Miss C. Rutter, Miss G. Temple and W. Jackson.

Royal visitors have always been made welcome to Chester-le-Street. Here we see George V and Queen Mary arriving at the Rural Council Offices in October 1928. Beatrice Smith from 8 James Street, Newfield is waiting to be presented to the Queen.

The Burns Infant School was in a very vulnerable position under the viaduct and this was one of the reasons given for its closure in 1940. Here we see a school group from the 1920s. Only one boy has been identified so far – second row, second right is T. Hornsby.

This photograph of Tom Gibbs and Mary Thomas in May 1924 shows them both in Salvation Army uniform. T.D. Gibbs was Clerk to Chester-le-Street Urban District Council from 1937. He started as a junior clerk in 1919 and from then on until December 1974 attended all committee and full council meetings. At that time he had been a Salvation Army officer for 51 years. He was President of the Rotary in 1956. Mrs Mary Gibbs was President of the Inner Wheel 1963-64, 1968-69 and 1977. For many years she was Chairman of the Friends of the Hospital and had been a Salvation Army songster for over 40 years.

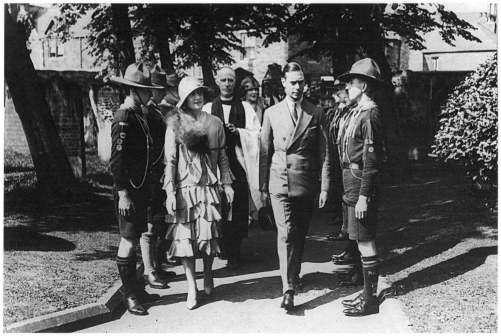

The Duke and Duchess of York arrive at the Parish Church to be greeted by Canon F.H. Jackson on 15th July 1928. The guard of honour was made up of the 2nd Chester-le-Street Scouts. The royal couple stayed at Lumley Castle – the guests of Lord and Lady Scarbrough.

Right: George William Horner. His factory was to expand in the 1920s from its base at Chester-le-Street to branch factories at London and Edinburgh with depots at Glasgow, Dundee, Berwick, Stockton and Hull. When Sheffield and District Retail Sweet association visited the works in May 1927 a souvenir booklet was published with the programme details of the visit. After being welcomed at Durham Station by George and Henry Horner and officials of the firm, they were taken by bus to the Guildhall for an official welcome. They then visited the Cathedral, Castle and Deanery. Luncheon was at the Rose and Crown at Durham. The party travelled to the Dainty Dinah factory and inspected its various departments, watched the manufacturing process and visited the beautiful garden area. Tea was in the Dainty Dinah canteen and later at 6.15 a special train waited for the party at the adjoining station at Chester-le-Street.

The breakdown crane specially constructed by Mr H. Leedale, Motor Engineer and Haulier of Picktree Terrace. (The site for many years of Picktree Coachworks.) In 1922 the crane was used for lifting over the parapet of the Lambton Bridge, at the bottom of New Bridge Bank, the remains of a lorry which had fallen into the River Wear. Leedale's garage in the 1920s advertises: 'Contractor to HM Government, HM Office of works, Durham County Council, Urban District Council etc. Estimates given for all classes of Haulage Salvage and Towage work.'

The town's children's outing leaving Osborne Road in 1926 during the Coal Strike which followed the General Strike. The first children's outing had been organised in 1923. Funds were raised in the town to cover expenses. Chester-le-Street was expanding rapidly in these years. The Urban District Council was building hundreds of Council dwellings, on the rising ground west of the railway station. The Urban Guide published in 1924 reads: 'It will be some considerable time before sufficient houses can be built to meet the requirements of the growing population.'

This advertisement comes from the *Chester Chronicle* of 3rd May 1925. Syson's, Percy Legg's, Dunn's, Tyler's and other shoe shops met the needs of the town and the surrounding area. Tulloch's and Pringle's were confectioners in the town. Miss Taylor's was a milliner; Doreen (L. Pinkney) was a hairdresser. This corner has changed very little in the 74 years since the advertisement.

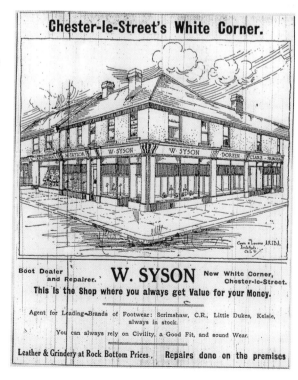

Chester-le-Street's White Corner.

Boot Dealer and Repairer. **W. SYSON** New White Corner, Chester-le-Street.

This is the Shop where you always get Value for your Money.

Agent for Leading Brands of Footwear: Scrimshaw, C.R., Little Dukes, Kelsie, always in stock.

You can always rely on Civility, a Good Fit, and sound Wear.

Leather & Grindery at Rock Bottom Prices. | Repairs done on the premises

This ex-works vehicle supplied in 1923 to Chester-le-Street Urban District Council by Mr B.K. Aunger, motor engineer of Chester-le-Street. The complete vehicle cost £600 or the chassis alone for £445. At this time a lot of hauliers and bus companies bought the chassis and used them during the week for haulage and at weekends for passenger transport. Ben Knight Aunger was a prominent businessman in Chester-le-Street. In 1921 he was advertising: 'Motor engineers and garage, all kinds of accessories stocked Newcastle Road and Agents for Angus Sanderson, Cubitt, Daimler, Kingsbury Junior and Vulcan Cars. Vulcan and W & G Lorries. Douglas, Enfield, Kingsbury and Triumph Motor Cycles.' Mr Aunger also composed and wrote religious songs and hymns. *Thy Debt is Paid* to the tune of St Elvan's (The name of his house in Tuart Street) has a chorus which ends: 'We there shall understand God's love so free.' Other members of his family continued the business until Jim Johnson took it over in 1966. This bill dates from the 1960s.

WEST ROAD, CROOK	AUNGER'S LTD	CHEAPSIDE, SPENNYMOOR
Austin, Morris, Wolseley, B.M.C. Commercials Phone: 70	Head Office: NEWCASTLE ROAD, Morris, M.G., Wolseley and B.M.C. Commercials. BY-PASS Hillman, Standard and Triumph. CHESTER-LE-STREET. A.A. Phone 2266. R.A.C.	Austin. Ford. Phone: 3180.

Miss Jackson   8, Newcastle Road, Chester-Le-Street.
Herald 5078 PT.   Job No. 113   P. 97

				F	0	C
Oct 18	Flush rad. fill bluecol, fit demister R/Window.				0	
	2½ Pints Bluecol				13	2
	Demister				16	6
				1	9	8

Chester-le-Street people and photographers of the century have recorded many of the events and happenings. However, it is often quite difficult to date photographs accurately. So please for historians in the twenty-first century, date and name the people on your photographs. These photographs were taken during the Carnival and Shopping Weeks held in the town in the 1920s and '30s. Parades through the town were a popular feature of these events. This parade beside High Chare shows the diversity and popularity of the parades. The two largest firms in the town, Northern and Horner's, were responsible for the organisation of the events. Floats such as Cosy Cafe and the Co-operative Insurance Society were typical of the parades. Cricket and football matches as well as races and tug of wars took place on the Deanery field. Profits and collections were usually for the Children and Old People's Fund.

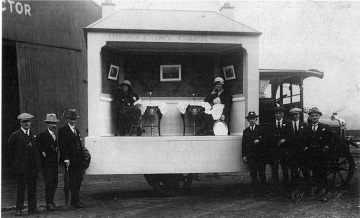

This photograph shows Percy Legg's leather shop on the left. On Shrove
Tuesday, Legg's was not barricaded with planks of wood but hides of leather
were strung over the shop front. Doggerels were printed on the leather. In 1920
the *Chester Chronicle* reports two rhymes.

You may go North, South, East or West   *Every man should tell his mate*
But if you pass this shop you pass the best   *That Legg's boot repairs are up to date*
When you think your boots are ended   *For many years they stood the test*
Bring them to Legg's and have them mended.   *So it stands to reason they are the best.*

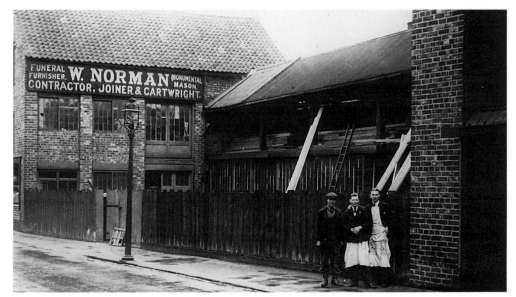

William Norman's firm – telephone number 29 – had been founded in the
1870s. This photograph shows Eric Baydon on the left and D. Hughes in the
centre. Norman's continued in West Lane until the early 1980s.

DEPRESSION AND RECOVERY

The riverside area was the centre for many summer activities. These boats were available for hire above Lumley Bridge. One of the Atkinson brothers also had a motor boat, which was available for hire at 3d for adults and 1d for children during the summer months. The service started in 1935.

The foundation stone for Chester-le-Street's new Masonic Hall was laid with full Masonic ceremony on 25th November 1931. Pictured here are: J.G. Finlayson, Cuthbert Wilkinson, Lord Ravensworth Provincial Grand Master for Durham, Colonel Woodbury Thompson and R.W.E. Dixon. Freemasons,

including the First Earl of Durham, had held their Masonic meetings since 1824 in the adjacent building to the Lambton Arms. Local architect A.H. Fennell supervised the building of the new Masonic Hall. The builder was Thomas Soulsby. It was officially opened November 1932.

The Atkinson brothers, Harry, Herbert, Harvey, George, Eddy and Ronnie are pictured here about 1935. Their father George Henry Atkinson served in the Boer War and in the mines before buying a horse drawn trap in 1908 to start carrying passengers between Pelton Fell and Chester-le-Street. He later set up the General Omnibus Service based in Osborne Road. In addition to daily bus

services, the company conducted private hire work and tours. The UDC guide for 1947 reads: 'The firm has built up a sound reputation for courteous and attentive organisation … and can be relied on for the best possible transport service to the public it serves.'

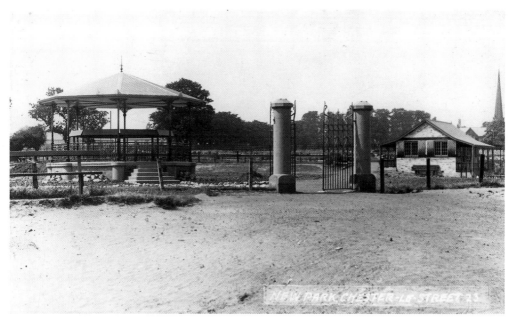

The idea of a town park had been suggested as a memorial to those who had died at the end of the First World War. However, it was not until the 1930s that the by-pass was constructed and the new park built. These photographs show the park as it was being developed. Mr S. Usher officially opened the park on the 12th May 1934. Attractions included several tennis courts and bowling greens and two putting greens as well as nicely laid out paths and flowerbeds. Illuminations were a feature of the town's Shopping Weeks. To celebrate the Coronation of George VI and Queen Elizabeth on 12th May 1937, the King's speech was relayed in the park followed by a grand display of fireworks.

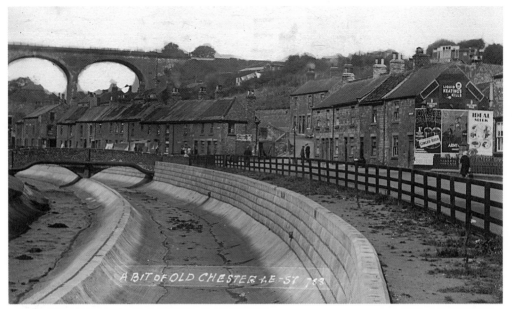

A BIT OF OLD CHESTER *.E-ST 783

The Cong or Cone Burn runs through the Burns. For centuries the Bridge End part of the town was really at the end of a bridge. The area had been an eyesore and the burn itself was described as a dirty smelling stream. Councillor J. Gibbs suggested concrete inverted arches be put in the stream so that it could be flushed regularly. The culvert through the area was constructed in 1931 at a cost of £10,000. A huge amount in those days! Seventy-five per cent of the work force was local men recruited from the large numbers of unemployed. These photographs taken at this time show the culvert and also that area known as Canada. This area belonged to the Lambton family. No reference has been found as to when it first became known as Canada but it is marked such on the first Ordnance Survey map of 1857.

Councillor Gilbert Robson Chairman of the Urban District Council officially opened the new Post Office in Front Street on 16th September 1936. The presentation key like the Post Office itself bears the insignia of Edward VIII. Only five other Post Offices in the country have this emblem. Guests at the official opening included P.G. Beaumont. Head Postmaster of Durham and Lieutenant-Colonel T.P. Hobbins CBE, Regional Director GPO North Eastern Region.

POST OFFICE, FRONT STREET, CHESTER-LE-STREET.

PROGRAMME

of the

OFFICIAL OPENING

of the

NEW POST OFFICE,

CHESTER-LE-STREET,

by

COUNCILLOR GILBERT ROBSON, J.P.,

(Chairman, Chester-le-Street Urban District Council).

Wednesday, 16th September, 1936,

at 2.30 p.m.

Programme

Guests will assemble at the new Post Office

at 2.15 p.m.

.. ..

P. G. BEAUMONT, Esq.,

Head Postmaster of Durham,

will introduce

LT.-COL. T. P. HOBBINS, C.B.E.,

Regional Director, G.P.O., North Eastern Region,

who will ask

COUNCILLOR GILBERT ROBSON, J.P.,

Chairman, Chester-le-Street Urban District Council,

to declare the office open.

.. ..

Afternoon Tea.

Lambton Castle, 1930. The Lambton family's first connections with Chester-le-Street are lost in the mists of time. Many members of the family, including Radical Jack and the Red Boy, were originally buried in the Lambton Vault at the Parish Church but their remains were re-interred in brick and concrete graves under the floor of the vault in 1920. The 1930s saw the deaths of the twin Earls within months of each other. Double death duties resulted in an auction of items from Lambton Castle. The auction lasted for fourteen days with 3,384 lots. The auctioneers Anderson and Garland still hold regular auctions in Newcastle today. The most famous, lot number 53 – Portrait of Master Charles William Lambton by Sir Thomas Lawrence (The Red Boy) – did not make its reserve price on the first afternoon of the sale 18th April 1932. Hence the Lambton family still own this now famous portrait. Later parts of Lambton Castle were to be demolished.

An advertisement for Harry Smith from 1936 reads: 'You require paper to wrap your goods then try Harry Smith wholesale Paper and Paperbag twine specialists. Blands opening – Paper and paper bags to suit all trades.' These premises in Edward Square had been built as a Primitive Methodist Chapel in 1860 but by 1886 it was described as, 'out of the way, out of date and as cold as the North Pole.' The Methodists moved to the schoolrooms on Newcastle Bank. The next we hear of the building is as one of the first cinemas in Chester – the Star Hall. The *Durham Chronicle* for the 7th October 1910 reports that plans were passed for a temporary veranda to the Star Picture Hall. A licence was granted in February 1911 but was not renewed in 1912. In 1983 the dark blue of the cinema ceiling was still visible. Harry Smith carried out his paper business here from 1922 to 1976.

This unusual photograph of harvest time in the 1930s shows an early Fordson metal-wheeled tractor and reaper cutting oats in a field near South Pelaw colliery. This tractor could have been supplied by C.F. Rymer Ltd (advertised right), formerly Huntley and Rymers. The garage was on the Front Street. It was later to become Young's agricultural division.

Broadway, Chester-le-Street 12847

There was much private house building in the 1930s. Wright and Kellett built semi-detached houses on Holmlands Park and on Newcastle Bank. Moles built the houses known as Wearvale Crescent (now 2-20 Newcastle Road) as well as some of Holmlands Park houses. While behind Newcastle Road, on the Broadway Estate, Hadrian Avenue was built by Wright and Kellett. William Leech was the builder of most of the houses in Broadway, Appledore Gardens, Tudor and Atkinson Roads. Note the signpost for Broadway.

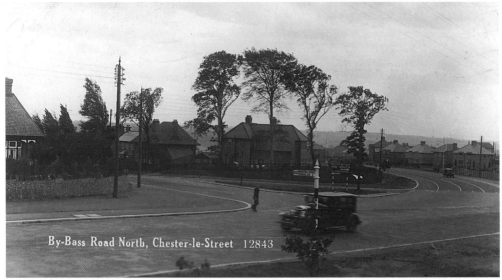

By-Bass Road North, Chester-le-Street 12843

The by-pass road, opened in January 1931. New houses known as Park Road South, Central and North were planned. This postcard was taken at the junction of North Road, Blind Lane, Park Road North and Newcastle Road. It was posted in 1937. The houses on Park Road North were still in the process of being built. Various local builders were involved. Don't look for the odd numbers 1-39 in Park Road North as they aren't there!

The traditional Shrove Tuesday football match continued until the 1930s. The advent of cars and buses as well as large shop windows meant that the game was doomed. Even before 1914, local papers talked of moving the game from the Front Street. The break during the First World War wasn't the end and despite yearly concerns it was not until 1929 that there was a serious movement by tradesmen to end the game. The Chamber of Trade gave three years warning that in 1934 they would not barricade their shop fronts and would involve the police if any property was damaged. February 13th 1934 saw a large police presence and although no game took place Pickles Mitchell a stout supporter of the game (pictured right) was arrested and taken to the Police Station. In 1935 the *Chester Chronicle* leader reads: 'It is now generally realised that the modern development of the town does not allow an annual rough and tumble fiasco in the main shopping thorough fare. Common sense has overruled custom.'

The year 1935 saw the Old Boys football team from Chester Grammar School touring Northern Ireland at the invitation of Mr J.J. Simm retired headmaster of the school who lived in Newcastle, County Down. Players included, back row: Horace Wadge, Ray Morris, T.W. Stoddart. Middle row: G. Johnston, R. Kirkbride, H. Hope, W.D. Hodby, A.S. Ward, J.E. Megoran, the referee is unknown. Front row: T. Scott, G.E. Burridge, H.G. Ward, J. Bell and A.C. Young. The *Chester Chronicle* reported: 'The Old Boys acquitted themselves handsomely and the tradition of the North-Eastern Amateur League of England was upheld in Ireland.' Harry Ward and Ted Megoran were to spend most of their teaching careers in the Church Schools of Chester-le-Street.

The Drill Hall was built in Picktree Terrace opposite the site of the Barracks in 1914. This photograph of a German gun (a trophy from the Great War) was taken by F. Price and includes Edward Price and his younger brother Terry.

The Co-operative Store dominated the lower end of town. The night of 19th January 1932 was to see the biggest fire in Chester-le-Street's history. Just before 6.00 am, T.W. Jobling, a boilerman at Horner's, saw flames and smoke at the rear of the premises and raised the alarm. By 7.15 the building was well alight and many people came from all over the town to watch the fire. Melted butter ran across the Front Street. There was estimated £100,000 worth of damage to stock and to the building. It was the worst County Durham fire on record. The photograph above shows the remains of the Co-op.

Right: The safe with its contents – Mr John Crawford, secretary of the society wearing glasses, is second right of the safe. The new premises designed and built by the CWS were opened 29th July 1933.

This view of the lower end of the street in the 1930s shows a busy town. In 1936 the honorary secretary of the Shopping Week, John Carver, wrote: 'Its position as the centre of a mining district is unassailable. Its markets (open and covered), its cinemas, its places of entertainment, its long street of up to date shops, the influx of people at the weekend, all go to prove the importance of Chester-le-Street.' Chester Cinema (later The Savoy) is on the right.

The Salvation Army has always placed great emphasis on music. In 1921 the Chester-le-Street Young People's Band was founded under Adjutant George Benyon by Bandsman Charles Slater assisted by Bandsman Billy Young. Under Mr Young the band travelled extensively. Pictured here is the band in 1934. The band played two solo pieces at the National Festival at Alexandra Palace in 1931 and 1935. The band also had many weekend engagements including places such as London, Belfast, Edinburgh, Nelson, Middlesbrough and many other cities. The photograph was taken in the yard of the Church School. Included are: Tom Coates, Wilf Smith, Ernest Cutmore, Stewart Stirling, Ted Wade, Tom Carr, Willie Hartley, David Neil, George Bowary, Band Sergeant Mr Elcoat, Band leader Billy Young, Arthur Rayburn, Jack Layton, Roy Shotton, Wilf Cutmore, Steve Elcoat, C. Morgan.

This photograph, taken at the Northern Bus Depot at Picktree Lane on 23rd December 1937, shows drivers, conductors and garage staff. Advertisements at this time offer 3 day trips to the Lake District and Blackpool for £3 10s and 5 day trips to North Wales for £7. Northern employed over 2,000 employees and more than 300 were employed at the Chester-le-Street depot (Urban Guide *circa 1934*).

This photograph of possibly Cairn's sweet shop at the Bridge End shows the gas lamp and a range of bottled boiled sweets and inside no doubt the full range of Dainty Dinah confectionery. The Horner enterprise continued to expand in the 1930s. The Urban Guide (*circa* 1934) states that: 'The large and wide distribution of this firm's goods has made Chester-le-Street a very familiar name to many thousands of sweet-eaters and their vans working from depots are to be seen from the North of Scotland to the South Coast of England.'

J.T. Saunders, who died 6th June 1933, was honorary organiser and fundraiser for many events in the town – he was missed by all. 'Mr Saunders could get money where nobody else could,' said J.G. Atkinson at a meeting of the town's Motor Ambulance Committee. Mr Grey went on to say, 'He wore himself out in his concern for the service and for other objects in the district for the assistance of the poor and needy.'

This window display, possibly for a competition during the Shopping Week in 1935 or 1936, belongs to J. Stoker Wholesale Confectioner. It includes products from Rowntree, Mackintosh, Needler's, Barker and Dobson, Cadbury's, Terry's and of course Dainty Dinah. Tradesmen who displayed a Red Spotting Competition badge had included some unusual article in their window, inconspicuously displayed. The object of the competition was to spot the greatest possible number of these articles. The prize was valued at 10 shillings and 6 pence.

THE WORLD IN CONFLICT

Lumley Castle, the former seat of the Scarbrough family was from the 1940s used by Durham University as a hall of residence. Pictured here in 1947 is the Baron's Hall of the castle. In the 1970s the castle became a hotel and staged its Medieval banquets in this same room.

This photograph taken at Chester-le-Street Secondary Modern School, Bullion Lane, on 18th December 1947 is autographed on the back by R. Muncaster, Ivy Grindle, Margaret Healer, Emmerson McMillan, James Fawcett, Joyce Smith, Pat Murray, Bryan Bean, Dorothy Francis, Clifford Searl and Nelson Lines. Unfortunately the ink for the last member of the group has faded and is unreadable. Mr Harker, the headteacher, did not sign!

Dressed for action! The Punshon family is pictured here on Front Street. Berets and hand knitted balaclavas, Siren suits, gabardine mackintoshes wellingtons and boots – ready for anything. The experience of the Great War meant that rationing was introduced soon after the outbreak of war in 1939. Butter, sugar, bacon and ham were rationed from January 1940 and clothes rationing was introduced in June 1941. Rationing did not finally end until 1954.

The Vagabond King in 1947 was a joint venture between the Chester-le-Street Operatic Society (formed 1903) and Cestrian Amateur Operatic and Dramatic Society (formed 1933). The two societies only this once in their histories joined. Pictured here are: Dennis Weatherley, Alan Kennaugh, Jack Warren, Bob Exley, George Dawson, Harry Fitzsimmons, and many other stalwarts of both societies. The production took place at the Empire Theatre. The theatre had been built in 1927 at a cost of £10,000. The Chester Picture House Company owned the Empire and two other cinemas at the end of the 1920s. The Smelt Organisation took over in 1934.

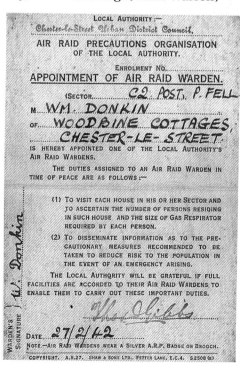

The proximity of Chester-le-Street to Tyneside and the Royal Ordnance Factory at Birtley meant that there had to be an efficient Air Raids Precaution system organised by the Urban District Council. Here is William Donkin's Air Raid Warden's appointment card issued in February 1942 with his duties. The ARP service was mobilised as early as the Munich crisis in 1938. Air Raid Wardens were issued with a silver ARP badge or brooch.

Fred Barber is pictured here with his motor bike. He is wearing the uniform of a Northern bus driver. Fred Barber developed the Chester Rest House (now The Lambton Worm), on North Road. The building was extended over the years as the Low Flatts, and Queensmere housing developed around it – as can be seen from the two photographs. Petrol rationing was in force from September 23rd 1939. Wartime slogans included: 'Make Do and Mend', 'Grow your Own Food', 'Dig for Victory' and 'Wage War on Waste'. These encouraged thriftiness and self-reliance.

Chester Rest House, Chester-Le-Street, County Durham.
Owner Fred Barber.

The Chester-le-Street Fire Station was based at the Urban Council's depot on Bullion Lane. T.W. Bathie is pictured on the left. A German bomb landed in the Hermitage Viaduct area in February 1941 damaging widows in the south end of town. T.D. Gibbs retained in his records a piece of the parachute's silk.

Compulsory war service meant that there was a shortage of miners and some who were called up for National Service ended up in Chester-le-Street working in local mines. December 1943 saw the first Bevin Boys, as they were called, go down the mines. Chester-le-Street's Bevin Boys are pictured here in a hostel at South Pelaw.

School dinners did not become a feature of school life until 1946. The *Church Magazine* for February 1946 reads: 'An excellent two course dinner is supplied for 6d, and in some cases free and the children can have as much as they like. The meals arrive in special containers in which they are kept very hot. Plates and dishes etc are all ready and warmed in the gas heated hot closet.' Miss Curry is seen here helping to serve dinners at the County Infant School. In April 1943 Councillor Patterson opened a British Restaurant serving meals for local people and children in the Central Methodist Schoolrooms. Seventy-two people could sit down at once and 300 meals a day were served.

Chester-le-Street Girls Training Company met at the Secondary School in Bullion Lane. The leaders were teachers from the various schools in the town and included Miss Knill and Betty Bush. This photograph, taken in 1943, shows 3 officers and 25 girls. Edna Bowman is on the right. She recalls braving the blackout to walk from her home in Hadrian Avenue to Bullion Lane.

The Working Men's clubs of the town played an important role in the social side of life throughout the century. This is a photograph of members of Osborne Working Men's club taken on a visit to Jeffrey's Brewery at Alloa in 1948.

They had travelled in an Atkinson's General bus. Members include: Ernie Cook on the extreme left front, Charlie Woodland is beside him and behind is Stevie Turnbull. 'It was a nice tasting beer and the great part of the group had quite a taste for it,' wrote Ernie Cook in the *Chester Post* in 1984. 'So much so that 8 of the members did not come back with the bus.'

This photograph of Chester-le-Street ARP (Air Raid Precautions) team shows Mr Bloomfield third from the left at the back. They are kitted out with tin helmets and blue overalls. Two buckets and a stirrup pump seem to be their only equipment! The 1941 report of the Co-operative Society reads: 'To those employees who voluntarily act as Fire Watchers etc upon our premises we tender our sincere thanks.'

The Chester-le-Street branch of the National British Women's Total Abstinence Union visited Brancepeth Castle 5th July 1949. Pictured here are, from the left: Mrs Jennings who lived in  the Caretaker's House at Station Road Chapel, Miss Richardson, Mrs Watson, Mrs McKeag, Mrs Atkinson and Mrs Elliott.

The Mobile Volunteer Ambulance Brigade is pictured here about 1940. Beryl Small is back right and third left, front row, is Peggy Dobson. Part time work became compulsory for all women aged between the ages of 18 and 45 in May 1943. The *Housewife* magazine for August 1940 has an article called 'Can I Get Work?' There is a quick survey of possibilities including the Women's Land Army; Navy, Army and Air Force Institutes or the NAAFI; the Auxiliary Territorial Service or ATS; Auxiliary Ambulance Service; Red Cross or St John Ambulance work either first aid or clerical; Women's Engineering Society or Munitions work; the Women's Auxiliary Air Force or the Women's Royal Navy Service. Florence Elizabeth Place, daughter of Thomas and Elizabeth Place of Chester-le-Street, a Petty Officer in the WRNS died 29th October 1942 and is commemorated in the Parish Church's Book of Remembrance and at the Cemetery. She was the only woman who died from the town in the Second World War.

This photograph of Chester-le-Street Secondary Modern School's staff at Bullion Lane was taken around 1949. It includes, back row: Bill Bulman, Isobel Brown, Eric Howard, unknown, Jack Ward, Frank Callan, Arthur O'Neil, Cecil Everett, Tom Haughan, John Kirkbride and the school secretary. Front row: Freda Potts (later Alderson), Peggy English (later Noble) Susanne Atkinson, Madge Knill, Jack McCulloch, Mr Tom Harker (head), Madge Taylor, Ella McCulloch, ? Goodchild, June Kendrew, Ellen Wilkinson.

Bus conductresses, or clippies, pictured in front of a Northern bus at the depot on Picktree Lane. Women, as in the Great War, filled the spaces left by the men on active service. The 314th Report of Chester-le-Street Co-operative Society in April 1941 reads: 'Already 44 members of our staff have been called to the colours and the society had to make many staff changes. Women workers have been engaged in many of our shops.'

Parades were a feature of wartime life. Probably used to break the monotony of wartime living, these photographs taken in the Burns area show the parade, which took place during 'War Weapons Week' in 1941. Colonel J.O.C. Hasted took the salute and with him were Sir George Morley Chief Constable and Alderman F. Nicholson. The final total raised during war weapons week was £73,996 17 shillings and 3 pence. 'Old blades make new guns' was the rallying call of a razor blade campaign run in the area in 1941. 110,582 blades were collected – enough to make 25 Bren guns, 40 rifles or 100 hand grenades.

Mary Bewick Wright married Jack (John) Mossop, 28th February 1942 in the Parish Church. Canon Appleton officiated. The wedding group was taken 3 days later in Newcastle. The photograph shows Mary in her white velvet dress (she later was to dye it black for dances), Jack, the bridesmaids Enid Wright on the left, Kathleen McLarverty on the right in their dresses of peach bloom velvet and the best man and groomsman Frank Gillan and Benny Kell. The reception was at the Colliery Inn, Pelton Fell. The landlord was John McLarverty brother-in-law to Mary.

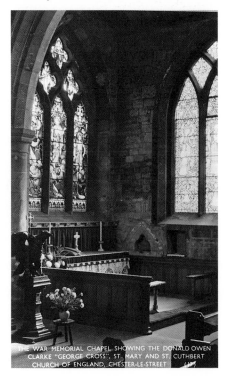

The Memorial Chapel at the South Aisle of the Parish Church is dedicated to Donald Owen Clarke. He was born in 1923 at Chester-le-Street, the son of Thomas and Bertha Clarke of Osborne Road. Donald attended Chester-le-Street Secondary School and joined the Merchant Navy as an apprentice. He died 9th August 1942 off Trinidad and was afterwards posthumously awarded the George Cross. The Civic Centre has a display of Donald's medals and details of his bravery. The Sea Cadets use the Donald Owen Clarke Centre at the Riverside. The Second World War Book of Remembrance lies to the side of the Chapel.

THE WAR MEMORIAL CHAPEL SHOWING THE DONALD OWEN CLARKE "GEORGE CROSS", ST. MARY AND ST. CUTHBERT CHURCH OF ENGLAND, CHESTER-LE-STREET

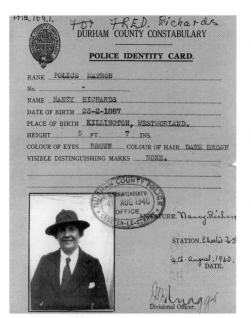

Above: Nancy Richards' Police Matron's identity card issued in August 1940 at the Chester-le-Street, Police Station. These were the days before women police and Mrs Richards was based in the town for many years. Her duties included escorting women prisoners and taking care of juveniles. She retired in 1952 with a pension of £109 15 shillings and 1 penny per annum. *Above right*: A letter from the Chief Constable.

Chester-le-Street 1507 Air Training Corps started as a Secondary School Squadron in 1941 and was open to all boys of the town and local area. Pictured here at camp at Pocklington Yorkshire in 1945, the cadets included: Back row: Richardson, Alan Usher, Harry Sowerby, Clarke, Owen, Haye, Beadle. Centre row: Coggins, Raymond Selkirk, Clish, Garner, Robson, Watson. Front row: Corporal Robinson, Flight Sgt Bolt, Pilot Officer Murray, Flying Officer Hedley, Flying Officer Foster, Flight Lieut Charlton, Flying Officer Davis, Flying Officer Taylor, Warrant Officer Yarwood, Drum Major Dowson. Seated: K. Dawson, F. Dawson, Mills.

Above: Chester-le-Street Regatta winners of the Jacob Hall Cup in 1949 were Walter Kirk, George Weatherley, George Armstrong, Bob Stephenson and seated Jimmy Armstrong. Jacob Hall was a long established jeweller in the town – advertising as early as 1883: 'Gold Medals, Silver Cups and other prizes suitable for Athletic Sports.' *Below*: George Weatherley in his skiff on the River Wear.

Clarence Terrace and Murray Road Nurseries opened in the 1940s. Here are
two photographs taken about 1949 at Clarence Terrace. *Above*: This group
included, back row, left to right: Mrs Proctor, Aveline Renwick (headteacher),
Mary Borradaile, Gwen Webb, Miss Laverick, Miss Moist and Winnie Watson.
Joseph Citrone (wearing the Fair-isle sleeveless jumper) is on the front row. He
did not like going to nursery and had to be carried from his home in Finchdale
Terrace. *Below*: Cod-liver oil was regularly given to the Nursery School
Children.

THE NEW
ELIZABETHAN AGE

Chester-le-Street's three Methodist Churches were well attended during the 1950s. Here we see members of Station Road Chapel on the steps after the service following the refurbishment of the organ. Members include: Mr and Mrs Davison, Miss Hann, Mrs Mary Yeoman, Sidney Yeoman, Tom Mowbray, Jim Puckering and his daughter Ruth, Mary Pointing who sang at the service, Mr Legg, Mr and Mrs Pointing, Hilda Coe, Lydia Hurworth with grand-daughter Audrey Coe, Billy Coe, Gavin Wilson, William Brown, Miss Jennings, Ethel Potts, Mrs Dora Curry, John Curry with grandson David Brown in his arms and Mr Stephenson the organist.

Lambton Terrace was built in two parts, this the lower part built in 1867 by John Kell. He decorated the houses with gargoyles. The stone with the date and name of the street had a griffin on one side and a monkey on the other. Hence the name Monkey Terrace. The

Grecian Lady graced the terrace until it was demolished for the road improvements by the hospital. These improvements were in place by July 1968.

Lady Lambton with her daughter Lucinda at a performance given by Edna Stewart's dancing class in the early 1950s. Edna Stewart had been the dancing instructor for the Amateur Operatic Society productions. The programme for the *Quaker Girl* in 1936 reads: 'The society is greatly indebted to Miss Edna Stewart for the arranging and tuition of the Speciality dances in this production.' In the same year Edna Stewart's Sunshine Girls gave a display in the Riverside Park as part of the Shopping Week.

Chester-le-Street Chamber of Trade celebrated the Coronation Of Queen Elizabeth the Second in 1953 with a window display competition. W.H. Dean the Newsagent, Stationer and Confectioner, in Co-operative Street won first prize for this display. The window display probably had some Horner's products. George William Horner had died in 1947 and Kenneth Horner now ran the company. A commemorative tin with the Queen's head on was produced for the Coronation. The company, however, increasingly faced problems and in 1960 the Official Receivers were called in and shortly after this the business ceased. The 'Five Acres of Sweetness' became a memory for Cestrians.

The top end of the Front Street, or High Front Street as it was known, just below the High Crown shows three well established tradesmen – Nixon's butchers shop (mentioned in Directories from 1906), Sowerby the plumber (from 1902) and Healer's fruit shop (from 1910).

Front Street's cobbles can be seen in the foreground of this photograph.
H. Greener started his newspaper shop in 1950s, it was continued by his son
Kenneth until the 1980s. Easiephit or Greenlees had been established since the
1920s. The doorway between the two shops led to Jubilee Yard where the two
Miss Blackburns baked for their tea-rooms.

New industries, such as D. & M. pictured here, came to the town. The London
Fashion House of D. & M. Cash, trading as Rodney Dresses, had started at the
Social Services Depot at Grange Villa with 60 men and women before moving
to the factory on Picktree Lane in 1947. The building had 22,000 square feet of
space intended for up to 500 workers – 'making dresses and frocks for the
country's overseas fashion drive.' Rodney's was to continue at Chester-le-Street
until the 1970s.

The cover of James Walton's autobiography *My Wild Friends* published in 1954 reads: 'The inhabitants of Chester-le-Street in the county of Durham have long ceased to regard with amazement the spectacle of one of its citizens going shopping accompanied by a fully grown  leopard. Little notice is taken of them for Mr Walton and his various four-legged companions are well known in the locality. Jimmy Walton writes in his preface: 'my first inspiration came at the age of 5 when my school teacher told me that wonderful story of Androcles and the lion – how I loved the idea of befriending and owning a lion.' These two photographs are proof that early ambition was fulfilled.

Chester-le-Street Riverside Park, taken one spring morning in the 1950s. A bowling match is taking place – please note the flat caps and trilbies. In 1955, to celebrate the 50th anniversary of Rotary, local Rotarians presented the park with a set of open-air draughts. The Urban District Council also built a new bandstand to mark the 50th anniversary of the Council the same year. In 1961 the UDC published a booklet called *This Is Your Town* and it tells us that the Council: ' … had made special efforts to increase the amenities by erecting a first aid room, pavilion extensions for bowlers and tennis players, purchased new playing fields, improved the children's paddling pool and not least continued the promenade for some hundreds of yards along the river bank.'

Left: Miss Minnie Curry and the County Infant School Christmas tree in 1953/4. Her helpers include: Hillary Clark, Pauline Warburton, George Nairn, Sandra Stanwick, Geoffrey Maughan, Elizabeth Spurr and, nearest to Miss Curry, Jacqueline Bates.

This school group taken in 1950 was prior to Miss Caroline (Carrie) Bonsall's reluctant retirement in December 1954. Miss Bonsall started as a pupil teacher at the Church School in 1905 at £6 per annum, then taught at the new Council Boys School from 1909. She later transferred to the Infant School when the schools were reorganised and remained there the rest of her teaching career. The Bonsall family were saddlers for many years in the town. Miss Bonsall died in 1975 aged 85 years.

Chester-le-Street County Infant School staff photographed in the playground in 1957 includes, back: Sadie Hall, Joyce Bates, Ceenie Newcombe, Margery Greener, Dorothy Raine, and in the front: Anna Goodyear, Paddie Hall, Miss Curry, Mary Atkinson and Doris Foster.

The Empire Ballroom taken from Osborne Road. The ballroom continued to be the meeting place for the young of the district. Ballroom dancing was popular until the advent of Rock and Roll.

The Empire Ballroom, all ready for a Valentine's Night special event – with prizes in front of the orchestra. The Empire Ballroom opened in 1928 and was famous for its floor with 200 springs. The theatre was behind the ballroom and was the venue for many local events. Kathleen Ferrier sang for the first time with Isobel Baillie at a Halle

performance of the Messiah here in December 1941. Schools held their Annual Prize Distribution or Speech Days at the theatre. Chester-le-Street Secondary Modern Schools in November 1952 included a scene from the *Merchant of Venice* and the school choir and orchestra. Barry Purdy and Doreen Taylor received Inspector Gargate's Prize for Good Manners and Courtesy.

Mary Robinson (née Tinkler) is seen here with the Empire Ballroom doorman, Mr Swinney, in about 1952.

The bus stop at the lower end of the Front Street, taken 11th December 1953 showing Hall the baker, Boot's, Leggett's, the Red Lion, Graves', Woolworth's and the Arcade. Hall's advertised: 'You'll enjoy a good meal at our cafe.' Graves' said: 'When in Chester-le-Street visit Graves' Cestrian Cafe for your luncheons and afternoon teas.' Whilst Leggett's reads: 'The hairdresser for good workmanship, cigars, cigarettes, pipes of the best quality tobaccos.' Arthur Leggett had been a prisoner of war during the First War and escaped in May 1918. He opened his shop at number 70 Front Street in 1919 and by 1938 was also at number 8. The barber's shop was to the rear of the premises. Leggett's continued as tobacconists at these premises until 1983. History repeats itself at number 8, in the 1990s with the hairdressers 'We're No Angels'. Woolworth's opened in 1927 and Chester-le-Street was the 267th branch.

The old Church Institute was the venue for most fund raising events. Pictured here is the St Mary's Guild stall with Canon and Mrs Appleton. The Guild began with concerts in January 1911 aimed at providing a piano for Sunday School classes. The girls centred their work largely on producing items for the Annual Sale of Work. Miss Kerrich-Walker used to check each item before it went on sale. The members used to clean the Church brass work and during the Second World War knitted garments for the troops.

Canon Charles Reginald Appleton in the Rectory garden. Jack Richardson, Curate from 1948 to 51, in his book *Jack in the Pulpit* writes about him: 'He was down to earth, a hail-fellow well met, with a word for everyone. He radiated a joy for living and as I look back I feel that he was as near to a true saint as anyone could ever have been.'

Graves the Bakers depot in Picktree Lane with its new fleet of vans supplied by Young's Motors. The other two photographs show the bakers shop at Front Street and the ballroom above. The Cestrian Dance Suite or the ballroom was the venue of many a newly married couple's reception. In the Church magazine for 1951 Graves' advertisement reads: 'Graves' Restaurant and Ballroom (also at Lambton Cafe at the corner of High Chare) for Morning Coffee, Luncheons and Teas, Banquets, Wedding Receptions and Dances.'

Graves' staff dinner dance took place in the ballroom. Pictured here are Chris Graves and his wife.

Willie Graves and his wife.

The Secondary Modern School Staff at Bullion Lane in 1959 includes back row: Joan Headlam (Patterson), Mrs Atkinson, Mary Dowson (Chapman), June Kendrew, Alf Hewitt, Cecil Everett, Margaret Barker (Emmerson), Mrs Young, Jack Fenwick, Bill Parker. Second row: Barry ?, Matt Raisbeck, Arthur O'Neil, George Bell, Alan Davison, ? Hill, Ray Naylor, Bill Geddes, Eric Howard, Bill Belford, Gordon Sutcliffe. Front row: Freda Potts (Alderson), Ella McCulloch, Tom Alderson, Peggy Noble, Bill Hedley, Mr Harker, Nell Leathard, Jack Ward, Ella Lowerson, Jean Copeman, Sheila Dixon. The school was now using the Practical Block in Low Chare and the Church Infant school in Middle Chare.

THE RACE FOR SPACE

Bullion Lane's football team from 1961-62 included, back row: Neil Peart, Bob Curry, Tony Swainston, Ken Massey, Ron Barrett, Thomas Hudson, Gordon McCann, Brian Ross. Front row: Billy Middlemas, R. Robinson, Michael McCann, Colin Todd, Harry Cole. The teachers were Bill Patterson and Ned Selkirk. Colin Todd was to have an illustrious soccer career – first with Sunderland before moving on to, amongst others, Derby County, Birmingham City and Everton. Colin also played 27 times for England. Since his playing days ended he has moved into coaching and management.

The Market Place taken in the 1960s. The Council run market was opened in October 1957. The UDC booklet *This is Your Town* reads: 'The gaily-covered stalls surrounded by bustling crowds are worth seeing. The Cong Burn has been covered in and a new roadway capable of carrying buses and other heavy vehicles has been constructed. Toilets have been built. South Burns and

North Burns have been transformed.' The booklet makes no mention of the removal of the town's war memorial to the churchyard. But a newspaper report talks of it having become a source of misbehaviour and a public nuisance. Fred Barber owned the Coffee Stall from 1927. Mr Michael was the tenant paying £14 per month rent. The Urban District Council placed a clearance order on the site and paid Mr Barber only for the land and building and nothing for the business and goodwill. On a Friday the Coffee Stall's takings could be £200. It closed in 1967.

The Allotments on Newcastle Bank are marked as such on the 1898 Ordnance Survey Map. This photograph gives a good view of the Northern Garage and Jack Wear's Post Office at Picktree Lane. Most of the allotment area was used for the Police Station (opened by Andrew Cunningham on 5th December 1969), the Magistrates Court (also opened on 5th December 1969 but by J.M. Black JP) and the Health Centre (opened in 1976). The Civic Centre was to be built here at the beginning of the 1980s and was opened in May 1982 by the Duke of Gloucester. The building is open plan (Burolandschaft). The 1985 Council Guide reads: 'It is an architectural expression of the ultimate in open Government.'

This view of Tates and Greenwoods dates to the early 1960s. The property above Tate's is to let by J.G. Usher and Son Estate Agents of 15/33 Middle Chare and this photograph was used to advertise this letting. Joseph Grundy Usher who died in April 1935 established Usher's in 1893. His son continued the

business. Leonard Usher was a Chester-le-Street Councillor, Deputy Lieutenant for the county of Durham and magistrate. He was widely known in Rotary and Freemasonry. He had been Colonel and Commanding Officer of the Home Guard and a founder member of the Chamber of Trade. C.F.C. Lawson said: 'Mr Usher was a gallant English Gentleman who served his fellow men to the best of his ability and that ability was high.' The fortnightly auctions in the upstairs room were for many an enjoyable day out. Peter Usher or Mr Wears as auctioneer, Mrs Millie Usher the clerk, Mrs Sheila Usher organising the lots with Gillian and Michael helping out in school holidays. Happy memories!

This photograph taken inside Crawford's Wool shop of Cone House 183 Front Street shows on the left Florrie Lamb and on the right Edna May Turner (née Crawford). Crawford's advertised in 1965: 'Everything for Baby, Wools and Haberdashery, Baby Linen and Tots Wear Our Speciality.'

May 20th 1969 was to see the 'Arcade' fire. The alarm was given at 6 pm and it was after 8 pm when the blaze was under control. 15 fire engines, 80 firemen with 15 pumps, 2 turntable ladders fought the blaze. The huge pall of smoke could be seen for miles. Jackson's the Tailors, the newsagents, Norman Wear's travel agency, Emmerson's furnishing store and the jewellers and fancy goods shop of S. Robinson and the offices above were all totally destroyed. Damage was estimated at £250,000. Major Roberts from the Salvation Army organised tea for the firemen. The building was demolished the next day. The Arcade was known as County House at the turn of the century and was the premises of first Pickering's, Hetherington's and later Armer's.

Harry Ward retired from teaching at the Victoria School in July 1968. Harry started and ended his career in the same classroom at the School but as he said had been other places in between! The photograph, taken in the Lambton Arms car park, shows a mixture of current and former staff and includes Elsie Ward, Dorothy Gall (now Hall), former head Lynn Turnbull, Peggy English, Wendy Johnson, Harry Ward, Jean Bates (née Harker), T.R. Laws (head), Mrs Kathleen Ward, Ted Megoran and Miss Lydia Roscamp. Six months earlier the Infants had moved to Hilda Park, the Juniors followed in January 1969. The Victoria's days as a school were over.

Mrs Stavers followed Miss Curry as head at the County Infant School and is seen here in 1968 with her staff. Back row: Elsie Ridley (auxiliary), M. Stephenson, Ann Willis, Margaret Robinson, Kathleen King, Mary Elliot, Kitty Collier, Jean Bates, Jean Campbell (auxiliary). Front row: Elsie Thirlaway, Mary Atkinson, Mrs Jan Stavers, Anna Goodyear and Sadie Hall.

This County Juniors boys' football team from the 1967-68 season is taken on the Burns football field. It includes Steven Ranson, Gary Jacques, Peter Harrison, goalkeeper is unknown, David Bulman and Keith Oswald. In the front row are: Andrew Veitch, Michael Gair, John Reach, Bryan Robson and Brian Robson. Bryan Robson went on to play for and captain Manchester United and England. He is in 1999 the manager of Middlesborough football club. His brothers Justin and Gary also followed football careers.

The Board Inn at the corner of Front Street and Low Chare had been in the Gibson family for many years. It was partially demolished in 1968, parts being reconstructed in Beamish Hall in the early days of the Museum. Some of the window framework can still be seen in Low Chare. The wooden decorations have been carefully painted to show the fruit.

The Kings Head opposite High Chare was closed in the 1960s and changed into a bank. The roofline is still visible above the new brickwork. F. Francis' shop was in the King's Head yard. The shop sold 'all the best makes of Sweets Chocolates and Tobacco, as well as fresh fruit and vegetables daily and soft fruit when in season.'

The old covered in market in July 1965 was now a pet and garden shop. The advertisements on the side show the changing entertainment scene of the 1960s. Gone was George Rowell at the Empire Ballroom. Monday was Teenbeat Nite, Friday was Cats Nite Out, and Saturday was Gear Nite. Dancing was by Disc Jockey to the Top Twenty although there were top line groups at all sessions. The Essoldo cinema stars included Tullullah Bankhead, Lee Marvin, Doris Day and Rock Hudson. The Queens was 'Now Open for Bigger Bingo every night at 7.30.'

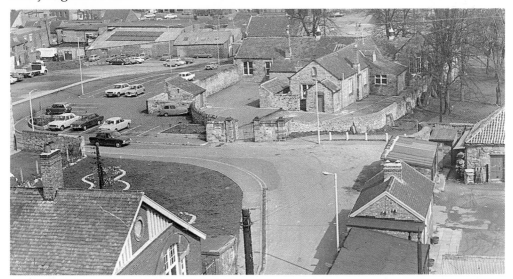

Taken from the Church Spire this photograph shows Church Chare. Thompson's yard on the right was then the base for a number of small businesses. It was cleared in the 1980s and the Anchorage Houses were built on this corner. The New Graveyard has been cleared and by the school wall can be seen the surviving headstones. The remainder had been used as the hardcore for the Riverside walk in the park. By this time most of the old housing in Middle Chare had been demolished.

The 1965 Wednesday Cricket team includes, Eric Henderson and Mathew Dennison. This was one of their last seasons at Chester-le-Street's cricket ground. The secretary for many years was Arthur Carver.

Boy Scouts at Church Chare School in about 1965. Unusually in that year there was a total of 12 boys due to receive the Queen's Scouting Award in the town. Here Colonel Sam Warwick, Chester-le-Street and District Commissioner, congratulates and shakes hands with Alan Bailey watched by back left, Ron Atkinson and on the right by Derek Pine and Alan Starkie.

Staff of Chester-le-Street Secondary Modern, Bullion Lane School with the headmaster Mr F. Lawson. Fred Donnolly took the surname of his wife Irene one of the three daughters of Jack Lawson (later Lord Lawson of Beamish and MP for Chester-le Street, 1919-1949). Fred had been a captain in the Royal Artillery during the Second World War. At the time of his death in 1985 he was Deputy Lieutenant for Durham County and had been a Labour Councillor for 20 years. Tony Golightly, Chief Executive of the District Council said: 'Fred Lawson was Mr Chester-le-Street. He was a marvellous man who always did his bit for the town.'

The Business and Professional Women's club taken in 1969 at the 25th Birthday dinner at the Red Lion. The photograph shows: Miss Esther Jackson, Miss H.E. Beaton, Miss Carr, Kathleen Howd and Miss Nell Leathard. The club was founded in 1944 and finally  folded in the 1980s. It met for some years in the Community Centre on Newcastle Bank and the 1975 programme includes: 'Wedgwood pottery by Mr Smurthwaite, Natural History by George Wall, a visit to the Police Headquarters as well as a Spring fayre, Summer outing and Christmas dinner.'

Chester-le-Street's Chamber of Trade are pictured here following a dinner dance in 1964. Back row: George W. Studham (Grocer, Weldon Terrace), S. Hall, G. Mohun, W.H. Dean (Newsagent etc, Co-operative Street), J. Marshall, Richard P. Hardie (Hire a coach of distinction for your outing, Newfield) and J.B. Stoker (Babyland, South Burns).
Front row: N. Earl, S. Hemingway (Manager for E. & A. Bell Newsagents, Front Street), N. Penny (Painter and Decorator, Newker Place), G. Shirwood, A. Emmerson (Emmerson's Arcade Stores complete home furnishers), W.P. Bennison.

1967 was to see the staging of the Church Restoration Committee's 2,000 years of history pageant at Lumley Castle. The pageant was to mark the Septecentenary of the Parish Church, 1267-1967. The brochure includes a 'History of Chester-le-Street' written by Mr H.W. Harbottle. This probably formed the basis for his book first published in 1976. Mr Harbottle was to form the local history society. His knowledge of Chester-le-Street's past was immense and all later local historians owe him a great debt of gratitude.

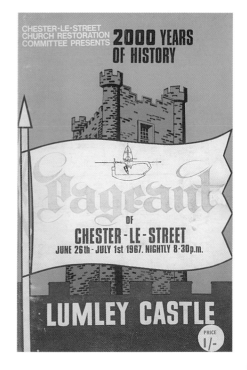

CHESTER-LE-STREET
CHURCH RESTORATION
COMMITTEE PRESENTS **2000 YEARS OF HISTORY**

Pageant
OF
CHESTER-LE-STREET
JUNE 26th - JULY 1st 1967. NIGHTLY 8·30p.m.

LUMLEY CASTLE

PRICE
1/-

Thomas Baxter White (fifth from the left), originally from Scotland, came as Confectionery manager to Graves in 1954. He won many Gold Medals at Olympia and other venues. Pictured here are the entries and prizes won by Tom Baxter White and his team and an Easter display in the ballroom. In 1965 Baxter White's was opened at the top of the Front Street. Mr White died in 1970 but the bakery shop has continued to bear his name.

Bridge End, Chester-le-Street in the snow in the late 1960s. The Central Methodist Church is seen here before its stone cleaning. The Mechanics' Institute taken over by the Urban District Council was renovated and reopened in 1966. Ye Olde Sweet Shop, the Chinese restaurant, Norman Richardson, the Granada TV shop were all part of the sixties scene. The first Citizen's Advice Bureau opened at the Mechanics' Institute in the 1960s. Noah Holyoake at the official opening expressed: 'The hope that local people would make full use of what he was confident would prove a helpful and valued service.'

TERRORISM, FAMINE AND STRIKES

The Queen's Silver Jubilee in 1977 was commemorated at Bullion Lane Junior Mixed School with this class 11 photograph. Back row: Miss Turnbull, James Dalrymple, Neil Suthern, Andrew Raine, John Hurst, Christopher Mallaburn, Graeme Affleck, Simon Norgate, John Start. Centre: John McGuffie, Steven Ramshaw, Stephen Ward, Shaun Murtagh, Diana Watts, Jacqueline Graham, Susan Quinn, Julie Chrisp. Front row: Rachel Thompson, Joan Burgess, Pamela Vest, Fiona Mountford, Debora Price, Lesley Alderson, Joanne Gordan.

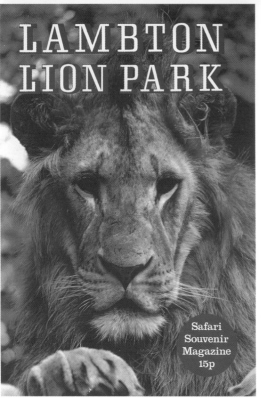

LAMBTON LION PARK

Safari
Souvenir
Magazine
15p

This is a photograph of the recently opened Lambton Lion Park in 1972. Lambton Lion Park, with its wide variety of animals, was a joint venture by the Lambton estates and the Chipperfield family. The concept of a drive-through wild life park was fairly new. Visting the 212 acres park and having baboons clamber over your car was popular. After some time it became Lambton Pleasure Park with an adventure playground and amusements near to the castle. It continued for a number of years in the 1970s.

Pelaw County Infant School teaching staff taken in 1977 includes: Caroline Ford, Dorothy Halford, Jean Gelson, Dorothy Hall Jean Evans, Peggy English, Anne Young (head) and Pat Jones. The School opened in January 1968.

Chester-le-Street Round Table in 1979 in front of Lumley Castle as Paul Sherratt hands over the chairmanship to Bill Metcalf. Others include: D. Robinson, N. McDonnell, W. Dryden, B. Walker, W. Norman, R. Redd, C. Brown, M. McCarrick, P. Burchall, H. Preece, J. Norman, D. Dick, K. Hutchinson, E. Brannigan, H. Bainbridge, J. Mulcahy, J. Tomlinson, J. Kearney, B. Nelson, B. Anson, G. Birkwood, D. Hughes, C. Oliver, G. Nairn, B. Simpson, F. Richards, E. Gilday.

Above: Floods at the bottom end of the Front Street have happened many times over the years. These *Sunderland Echo* photographs taken in March 1979 show local ladies being rescued.

Left: This further picture of the 1979 floods shows the doorway of the Red Lion. The Red Lion had taken the place of the Empire Ballroom and Graves' Ballroom as the venue for dinner dances, ladies' nights and wedding receptions. There was also a regular Saturday night dinner dance.

St Mary's House from the Front Street. It was demolished in 1982. The car park at the rear led to the Black Path, which ran from Co-operative Street to Market Lane. There was a tyre factory here for some time. H. Young (Motors) Ltd had taken over the Horner's site in 1964 and from here ran their motor and agricultural vehicle firm. Young's had been founded in 1923 by Henry Young. Young's garage at the top of Front Street was the main Ford dealer in the area. In 1955 there were branches at Sunderland, Darlington and Newcastle.

St Mary's House taken from the rear of the premises was the Urban District Council and from 1974 the Chester-le-Street District Council Offices until the new Civic Centre was built. The shapes cut in the turf are the footings for the Housing Department's temporary offices.

Chester-le-Street's Union and Guardian Offices were the premises used by the Rural District Council. After 1974 the District Council continued to use the offices until the new Civic Centre was built. Pictured here are: Councillor Malcolm Pratt (South Pelaw), Councillor Dr Hugh Mackay

(North Lodge), Tony Golightly (Chief Executive of the District), Chairman of the Council, Councillor Joe Bickle (Sacriston), and Councillor Violet Stewart (Pelton) with the plaque from the Union Offices (1899) in about 1979.

W.A. Carver Gents Hairdresser. Carver's is first mentioned at 1 Low Chare: 'Ladies and Gents' Hairdresser – Bobbing and Shingling a Speciality' (*Chester Chronicle*, 1927). Arthur Carver was to join his father at the age of 14. The business was later to be at 187 Front Street, Low Chare and Bridge End Chambers (1938). Doris Carver, his wife, ran a hairdressers for many years at 2 Picktree Lane. By the 1980s Arthur's shop was a warm haven for many of the old timers of Chester-le-Street and when the *Chester Post* was being published many an argument about Chester's history was thrashed out in his shop. Arthur finally retired in April 1989.

Arthur Carver is seen here receiving the Silver Acorn from Chief Scout, Sir William Gladstone, in 1974. 'Skipper', as he was later known, was a founder member of the 2nd Chester-le-Street Scout Group. In 1922 he had joined 1st Chester-le-Street as a wolf cub. In 1927 he transferred to the 2nd group. In 1930 Arthur took out a

warrant as assistant scout leader. He was appointed scout leader in 1933. He went on to receive medals of merit, long service badge then a bar to his merit medal. Following his compulsory retirement from active scouting of 55 years in 1977, he was made life president of the scouting group. The Burns School was the meeting place for the 2nd Chester-le-Street Scouts and in 1978 the name was changed to Carver House to thank Arthur for his years of service to the movement. In 1980, Chester-le-Street Rotary named him as the recipient of the First Good Citizen of the year award. 'The youth of Chester-le-Street were always amongst the highest priorities in his life.'

Chester-le-Street Model Engineering Society has model train tracks in the park. In 1970 they were having problems with vandals. Pictured here are Mervyn Vest, secretary, Arthur Snaith, George Nairn and K. Challoner who were repairing the tracks.

Pictured in the garden of St Mary's House, the last Urban District Councillors and Council officials on 31st March 1974. Back row: C.F.C. Lawson, T. McHugh, A. Golightly, J. Knox, P. Usher, J. Willis, Jack Cunningham (later a Member of Parliament and Cabinet Minister), W. Dean, N. Lamb, R. Bone, M. Pratt and Howard Thomas. Front row: Tom Davison, W. Gowland, Mrs D. Riddell, N. Riddell and T.D. Gibbs..

John Thompson shows pupils from Chester-le-Street Hermitage Secondary School the site in his builders yard, Church Chare, where they were hoping to dig for Roman remains, October 1974. However, the Department of the Environment stopped them and a team from Durham University dug the  site. To make up for their disappointment Mr Thompson gave permission, under the supervision of their teacher Brian Tebbett, to dig in some gardens opposite his home on Mains Park Road. Hermitage School moved to North Lodge from Bullion Lane in about 1970. The school moved again to new buildings at Whitehill following reorganisation of Secondary Education in the area in 1976.

Chester-le-Street Hospital Drama Group was formed in 1969. Its aim 'not just to gain personal satisfaction from participating in the many aspects of drama but also to entertain and bring pleasure to other people in the community.' Any money raised was donated to buy items for the welfare of the patients. Here is one of their productions. Now in 1999 they are joined with West Pelton Drama group as the Nomad Theatre Company. This photograph is from the production *Pools Paradise* in 1972. Katherine Barker is on the left, Colin Smith centre and Joyce Whitmore is on the right.

The Hermitage School staff pictured at North Lodge in 1970 includes, back row: Arthur Barron, Brian Tebbitt, unknown Australian, David Greaves, John Jackson, Andy Storey, Colin Bewley, John Attis. Second row: Margaret Caygill, Leslie Milner, Tom Craggs, Ed Ramsey, Leslie Ball, Jeff Denton, Ed Selkirk, Charles Bradshaw, Bill Ardle, Marilyn Gales, Rita Barron. Front row: Ann Simpson, June Kendrew, Mary Hammel, Ann Richardson (Nelson), Jean Copeman, Mr Lawson, Eric Howard, Ann Curry, Betty Grieveson, Jean Kinghorn, unknown.

A. Hedley Tyres commenced business on 5th July 1971 in a small workshop located at the top of Clifford Terrace. Alan Hedley had previously been employed with H. Young (Motors) Ltd. In 1973 the business re-located at Devon Crescent, Birtley and by 1976 was employing 16 people. The company later diversified for a short time into passenger coaches. In 1983 Hedley's moved to Stella Gill and have continued there since. These photographs are from the early days of the company.

GLASNOST AND PERESTROKIA

1st Chester-le-Street Girls' Brigade Company celebrating their tenth birthday in 1987 at Chester-le-Street Methodist Church.

The 2nd Chester-le-Street Scout group taken in February 1984 in Carver House prior to the annual Gang Show. The scout leader is John Lewis who died at an early age in 1992. He received the Silver Acorn in 1988.

The committee and founder members of North Lodge WI taken at their 21st party in December 1982. Back row: Maud James, Maureen Martin, Maeve Waggott, Joan Sears, May Alderslade, Edith Dent, Joyce Whitmore. Front row: Joyce Reed, Jean Gelson, Irene Harding, Olive Murrell, Audrey Norris, Louise Earnshaw, May Cudworth.

The new Parish Centre was built on the site of the old school and was officially opened in December 1987 by the Bishop of Jarrow Rt Rev Michael Ball. This photograph was taken during the construction of the centre in 1987. It is now a busy place. The Parish Office is based here. The monthly craft fairs are popular events and are well attended. The lunches are greatly appreciated by all.

The Parish Institute had been the centre of the Church's social life since it opened in December 1891 and was the venue for many events. By 1986 however it 'was shabby and ill equipped to serve our present needs.' The buildings were demolished in January 1988. Another piece of Chester-le-Street gone. However, the removal of the Institute opened up a new vista of the Parish Church. The Church stands in all its splendour and beauty as probably never before in its history. The District Council has provided flood lighting, which makes it even visible at night.

The Five Acres of Sweetness of
G.W. Horner's Dainty Dinah works
had by the 1980s become an area
for development. Much of the site
was still recognisable to old
Horner's workers and parts of the
factory had changed little. There
was still to be found under loose
floorboards and in roof spaces
signs of Horner's and even wooden
boxes printed with Horner's
predecessor's name 'The Stag
Steam Works'. These photographs
show the 1920s chimney, 106 feet
high with its tiled Dainty Dinah
and the bust of Dainty Dinah
which to many Cestrians travelling
by train meant home.

Left to right: Deaconess Edna M. Bell, Rev Derek Aldridge, Rev Walter Best and Ernest Armstrong MP. The 1960s and '70s had seen talk of the Church of England and the Methodist Church joining. It was in 1978 that the three chapels in Chester-le-Street amalgamated. The Durham Road and Station Road premises were sold and the Central Chapel became the Methodist Church in the town. There were sweeping changes in the chapel itself. The old pews were removed as was the original pulpit and communion area, newly painted it presented an up to date face to the united members. In 1980 Ernest Armstrong MP, with a Methodist background, opened the new Church.

Right: The cover of a brochure for the opening and dedication of the Methodist Church extension by Paul Bartlett Lang, secretary of the Joseph Rank Benevolent Trust, 9th April 1983. The hall was in 1985 later named the Walter Best Hall in memory of the minister 'without whose energy and initiative the scheme would never have started.'

CHESTER-LE-STREET METHODIST CHURCH

THANKSGIVING SERVICE

TO CELEBRATE THE
OPENING AND DEDICATION
OF
NEW CHURCH EXTENSION
2.30 p.m.

SATURDAY, 9th APRIL, 1983

The clearing of the Horner's site also included the Victoria School and these shops in Market Lane. There had been a market here at the turn of the century. North East Antiques used these premises before they moved to Ashley Terrace. Local Historian Gavin Purdon also sold militaria and other items from here. The name has been retained but nothing now remains of Market Lane.

A number of fine houses in the town changed in the 1980s. Wearvale on Newcastle Road was demolished and houses built on the site; Castle View, on the hill above, had new housing built in the grounds; The Grove and The Rectory became offices; West House on West Lane was turned into a Nursing Home (pictured here) as was Durham House on Mains Park Road. Mains House which stood empty and derelict on the corner of West Lane and the Front Street, was finally demolished and new offices and shops built on the site.

1983 saw the 1100 Celebrations of the arrival in Chester-le-Street of the monks carrying St Cuthbert's remains, not only the Church but also the whole town celebrated for a year. Many different events took place including a road run, first day covers, a youth pageant, a pilgrimage to Holy Island, a visit from BBC's *Down Your Way*, lectures and special services at the Parish Church. This photograph shows the North Lodge WI handing over to Councillor Pratt the six foot long embroidered tapestry they had worked on. The tapestry represented in stitches different aspects of Chester-le-Street's history. It was designed by Edna Sanderson and included the needlework of 33 members. The tapestry now hangs in the Civic Centre, nearby are the details of each member's contribution.

The Chester-le-Street Fun Run planned to have over 2,500 runners as part of the 1100 celebrations. It was organised by the Chester-le-Street Athletics Club and leaders from Park View Community Association. The run took  place on 30th May 1983 and followed a five and a quarter mile course. The runs continued in the years following and Steve Cram is pictured here in the Bullion Hall area.

The 1980s were to see Chester-le-Street Co-operative Society celebrate 125 years of existence and then be swallowed up by the North Eastern Co-op. In August 1987 there were celebrations of 125 years and much mention of Chester-le-Street as the last surviving independent Co-op in the North East. The booklet here was issued and included a history as well as photographs. January 1989 saw the merger and plans for a Co-op Superstore at the top of St Cuthbert's Walk, although the existing premises were retained. The new superstore opened in January 1991. The North Eastern Co-op promised 'to preserve and enhance co-operative trading in the town.'

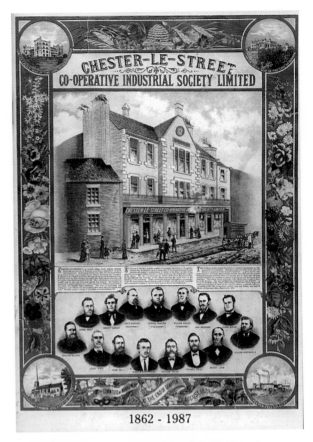

1862 - 1987

This photograph, from 1988, shows the re-enactment of Charles Wesley's visit to the town, as part of the 250th celebrations of his setting up of Methodism. The Rev Eric Mason as Charles Wesley is riding on a horse lent by Coppy Farm Beamish led by Bill Gilhespy and his daughter, Valerie Swinburn.

St Cuthbert's Catholic Church was Re-Ordered in 1984 – that is updated in design to conform to the present thinking of the Universal Catholic Church (left). The consecration of the Church and the dedication of the New Altar by Right Rev Owen Swindlehurst, Bishop of Chester-le-Street, Auxiliary Bishop of Hexham and Newcastle, took place 29th November 1984 (above).

Two classes at Cestria Primary school in 1988. The head, Paul Thompson, is on both photographs. *Above*: The teacher is Mr Shields. Back row: Christopher Jones, Carl Thompson, Steven Carr, Billy Musk, Ewan Mattheys, Mark Cranston, Paul Wilson, Gary Walklate, Jamie Armstrong. Middle row: Daniel Magdalana, Richard Hall, Nicholas Brown, Ian Collinson, Nicola Illingworth, Claire Hall, Paul Richmond, Peter Collinson, David Graville, Shaun Moon, Chris Watson. Front row: Phillipa Rothwell, Layla McMullen, Emma Robinson, Rosalyn Graham, Tracy Wilson, Katie Lanigan, Kirsty Dixon, Carolyn Redpath, Emma Fulton. *Below*: The teacher is Mrs Muxworthy. Back row: David Reed, Paul Clark, Ben Tilley, David Kershaw, Matthew Wood, Steven Walklate, Richard Nichol, David Weatherspoon, Jonathan Dent. Middle row: John Marshall, David Fox, Lee Scroggins, Paul Smith Lindsay Farthing, Lesley Ann Cranston, Laura Kershaw, Kate Mattheys, Gillian Hall, Rebecca Powell, Christopher Richmond, Lloyd Pennock, Peter Mullinger. Front row: Jenny Hutchinson, Susie Lavery, Jane Ibbertson, Helena Gilbert, Leanne Dawson, Laura Foster, Gemma Metcalfe, Alison Brown Laura Brown.

TOWARDS THE MILLENNIUM

Pictured in the St Cuthbert's Walk car park are Josie Citrone and his mother Mary. The St Cuthbert's Walk complex, with its alleyway of covered shops leading from the Front Street to the Co-operative food store, was opened in 1991. It featured until 1999 the famous statue of Dainty Dinah from Horner's factory. Bryan Robson officially opened the mall.

The 1980s had seen a new and growing interest in Chester-le-Street's past. Exhibitions held by the Heritage Group, were well supported. A 'Trail around the Town' and 'Chester-le-Street in 1851' were published by the group. Two books of postcards were to follow. There was a keen interest in G.W. Horner and his factory. In 1990 Gavin Purdon's book *It Was Grand Toffee* was launched at the town's library with a number of different events including an exhibition of photographs and memorabilia (right). Pictured here is: Alice Scott, Jackie Edwards, a member of the library staff dressed as Dainty Dinah and George Daniels composer of the *Dainty Dinah Waltz* in September 1990.

Sweet Memories of

GEORGE W. HORNER & CO., LTD.,
Manufacturer of Confectionery Specialities
CHESTER-LE-STREET
COUNTY OF DURHAM

**in
CHESTER-LE-STREET LIBRARY**
from
6th September - 6th October 1990

DURHAM COUNTY COUNCIL
COUNTY LIBRARY

Cestrian Flower Club held its 25th Anniversary dinner at Lumley Castle on Friday 24th June 1994. The guest speaker was Rev William McMillan. The photograph includes, from left to right: Judy Wanless, Jean Suggett, Rev McMillan, Mrs Campbell, and Nancy Wilkinson

Lumley Bridge continued to support the increasing traffic of the 1990s until problems were discovered and a traffic light system was introduced in 1995. The bridge, opened in 1914, was not made for the 11,000 cars a day it now had to carry. A new bridge was built up river from the original site. In November 1997 the Prime Minister opened the bridge and is pictured here planting a tree to mark his visit.

The Riverside Park remained much the same as it had been when it was opened in 1934. The 1990s were to see major reconstruction and the removal of many of the old features of the Park. The rose beds and the owl statues, the band stand, the car parking area off the by-pass and the tall privet hedges all went. The pavilion seen here was replaced with the Park Centre and a new garden area called the Riverside Garden was developed. The paddling pool and children's play area were relocated and fenced off. The Riverside is a popular place and many families enjoy a day at the park.

Chester-le-Street Golf Club was formed in 1908 on the Lumley estate with a nine-hole course. It has continued on the same site since then. There have been over the years a number of club houses starting with an ex-army hut. This photograph shows the old club house has been demolished to the far left and the new club house was built and combined with the modern extension here. The completed club house was officially opened by the Earl of Scarbrough in 1998. The course has also changed over the years, extended to 18 holes in the 1960s and in 1995 the club exchanged part of the course for land on the New Haughs.

Red Rose School celebrated 75 years in 1996 with a week of events and a service in the Methodist Church. Planned in the 1910s it was not opened until 1921. Named after the Red Rose Estate it was built on, the school has had a number of heads including Agnes M. Prest, Miss Selkirk, Mr Kirkbride, Gordon Cooper, and the present head Judith Lees. Here are children dressed up for the 75th celebrations.

A group of children in the school yard.

The Queen accompanied by Prince Philip opened the Riverside development in October 1995. These photographs of that day were taken by the Mike Blenkinsop Studios and record some of the main events of the day. Here, the Queen is introduced to Tony Greensmith, Chief Executive to the District Council. Also pictured is Councillor Malcolm Pratt

Councillor Ron Trotter of Chester-le-Street District Council welcomed the Queen to Chester-le-Street.

Earlier the Royal car was greeted by Cestrians at the lower end of Front Street. This was of course before the Front Street was closed to most traffic in February 1998.

Mary Mossop was awarded the MBE in the Queen's birthday awards for her services to the people of Chester-le-Street. She is seen here with her son Alan and his wife Pamela on the 12th November 1996 at Buckingham Palace. Mary is a living history book and shares her knowledge of Chester-le-Street's past with anyone who expresses an interest. Her scrapbooks and memories have assisted the compilers of this book. Thank you Mary.

Tommy Moffat pictured here with his wife outside Buckingham Palace after receiving his MBE. Other recipients over the years include: George Battensby, Cissie Wilkinson, Minnie Curry, Jack Layton, Tom Dunn, Gordon Maule, Malcolm Pratt and Dr Hugh Mackay.

Park View School's Year 13 (Second Year VIth) pictured in 1998. Front row, left to right: Kay Ingleby, Tracey Scott, Suzanne Stirling, Lesley McGoldrick, Mr Veitch, Mr Watt, Ruth Barron, Leanne Carr, and Becki Powell. Second row: Jenny Hutchinson, Lindsey Brannen, Laura Brown, Lisa Murphy, David Giles, Gillian Denny, Hayley Reynolds, Nadine Bainbridge, Claire Wake, Katie Woodhead, Emma Hardy, Gillian Hall, Laura Thomson, Alex Ottosson, Lisa Horsley, Cheryl Thompson, Jane Ibbertson Richard Todd. Third row: Richard Brown, Louisa Jordison, Danielle Buxton, Keighley Potts, Rachel Heaver, Emma Gillis, Rachel Lynch, Stephen Hall, Katherine Mordue, Kate Mattheys, Laura Kershaw, Andrea Smith, Sarah Gibbons, Neil Robinson, Claire Cowie. Fourth row: Rachael Skirrey, Allison Lonsdale, Angie Crossley, Andrew Gregg, Paul Denton, Stewart McCallum, Ian Miller, Marc Horn, Simon Mudd, Anthony Routledge, Christine Heslop, Lindsay Wilson, Helen Thompson, Gary Blair. Fifth row: Helena Gilbert, Simon Cullen, Paul Smith, Ian Thompson, David Kershaw, Paul Clark, David Osfield, Peter Spencer, Lee Scoggins, Lap Keung Chui, Vicky Peverley. Back row: Kieran Raine, David Hudson, Stewart Doyle, James Brown, Scott Seaton, David Joel, David Potter, Chris Newman, Philip Gosling

This photograph taken in 1990 of the Bridge End surgery shows the breeze blocks already for the new building. The surgery built in the 1950s was one of the first purpose built surgeries following the National Health Service's conception. Dr Myles Hutson had first practised from the house and surgery just below the Lambton Arms. He built a house on Newcastle Bank. The name Chalmers Orchard recalling the origins of the Bridge End site. Dr Hutson was to die before the new surgery was opened. Margaret Hutson officially opened the building dedicated to her husband's memory in February 1991.

Kamp Lintfort and Chester-le-Street became twin towns in October 1981. The charter is on display in the Civic Centre. Various visits have been made over the years. This photograph shows a visit organised by Park View school in the mid 1990s.

This photograph was taken at the 50th Charter Anniversary of Chester-le-Street's Inner Wheel in 1994. Taken at the United Reform Church are: Millie Usher, founder President, Alan Cutty, the President of Rotary 1994, Nancy Stoker the President of Inner Wheel 1994, Mrs Alex Cutty and Jack Stoker a former President of Rotary.

Don Robson (chairman), Ian Caller (president) and Tommy Moffat (director) of the County Cricket Club celebrate First Class County Cricket at the Riverside. The first cricket at the Riverside took place on 2nd August 1994 with a Second X1

Match against Middlesex. *The Times* correspondent Sir Clement Freud reported of the ground: 'It is bigger than the Oval, flatter than Lord's, greener than Trent Bridge and unlike existing county grounds, this one is to be the jewel in the crown of a wondrous new 150 acres leisure development in the shadow of Lumley Castle.' The main pavilion, with hospitality boxes, bar, function suites and meeting rooms also has seating for 3,000 spectators. Additional stands will eventually mean that the ground will have a capacity of over 14,000.

Margaret Jane Willis was born in Chester-le-Street 27th January 1887. In 1914 when war was declared she went with her older sister Mary to Newcastle and 'Took the King's Shilling'. She joined the Queen Mary's Army Auxiliary Corps and went down to Folkestone for training. In February 1915 she was stationed at Beaumaris France. She stayed there in a variety of occupations until 1918. Beaumaris was where she met and later married Company Quarter Master Sergeant Walter Frederick Cranfield. A founder member of the British Legion in Leicestershire, she was actively involved with the Movement. In the Second World War she joined the ARP and was known as 'The Gas Mask Lady'. In 1999, at the age of 102, Margaret Cranfield was awarded the Legion d'Honneur in the class of Chevalier (Knight) for her services to France as an allied soldier fighting on French territory in the First World War.

Crocodillos is a Mecca for the young of Chester-le-Street. Few who dance the night away realise that they are following in the footsteps of other Cestrians. Graves' Ballroom was its predecessor. In the interests of history, George Nairn and Dorothy Hall went to the night club just before it opened its doors to see what remained of the past. Nothing could have been further from the Ballroom. The purple and gold decoration and the gilt chairs were of the present! Pictured here in 1999 are three of the bar staff: Johnny, Claire Hall and Alexis.

The following photographs are from a display hanging in Chester-le-Street Town Football Club. The display features many of the Chester lads who have gone on to play football for some of the most famous clubs in the land.

The Robson brothers – Bryan (West Bromwich Albion, Manchester United, Middlesbrough), Garry (West Bromwich Albion, Gateshead) and Justin (Gateshead, Durham).

Clockwise from top left:

Gordon Hughes – Newcastle and Derby County.

Alan Suddick – Newcastle, Blackpool, vice-president of Chester-le-Street Town FC.

Paul Atkinson – Sunderland and Port Vale.

Joe Bolton – Sunderland and Middlesbrough.

Newcastle's Albert Bennett heading the ball against West Ham United at St James' Park in the 1960s.

Back row, centre: Robert Thursby – Bishop Auckland, captain of the English Amateur International side and Middlesex Wanderers.

Barry Endean – Watford, Charlton and Blackburn.

Station Staff at the turn of the century.

'Chester-le-Track' staff at the official launch in 1999. Back row: Alex Nelson, director and station master, Steve Robson, director, John Partridge, director. Front row: Derek Ellis, clerk, Helen Gray, shop manageress, Stuart Gray, clerk.